Breakthrough
to a
Supernatural
LIFE

Keys to Hearing God's Voice

FRANKLYN M. SPENCE

xulon PRESS

Dedication

◆—————◆

irstly, this book is dedicated to my friend and King, Jesus Christ. The reality of a living, breathing Jesus showing up in my life has changed me and molded me in every way. What he has done for me is so much more than what I could ever do for him. Thank you. Jesus, please accept this book as an offering to you for the building of your kingdom.

The working of the Holy Spirit—his inspiration and guidance—has been instrumental in my life, and this book has been directed and inspired by him. To get to know him in even a small way is life-changing. Just the thought that he would leave the comforts of his home in heaven to come and live in me fills me with awe. Thank you, Holy Spirit, for speaking through me in this book.

And the love of Father God motivates me to strive and reach out with his message, even when I'm more comfortable hiding away. May we all know you better. Thank you for interrupting my comfortable existence when I was sixteen years old!

I would like to thank my dear friends and mentors Jacques and Jo-Anne Leroux. Years ago they didn't know me from anyone, but when they prayed the Lord spoke to them and told them to give me a chance. They believed in me before I believed in myself. They mentored Amy and myself, even when it hurt. Jacques and Jo-Anne pushed me into public speaking, preaching, teaching and relying on the presence of the Holy Spirit. With no track record and no experience, they invited me to be a regular speaker at their retreat center. Everyone who came to those early conferences will be forever touched by the presence of our most wonderful Lord and Savior, but no one more so than myself.

I'd also like to thank Apostles Russ and Mave Moyer at Eagle Worldwide Ministries in Hamilton, Ontario, Canada. They have been pioneers in the area of the prophetic movement and working with the Holy Spirit, and the training and mentoring I received from them helped me spread my prophetic wings.

Thanks to Dan and Dale Rosborough and the folks at the Tent of David Church, who have been a continual source of love and support on my journey. Thanks to Bill Carruthers, whose constant support and encouragement has meant so much to me over the years. And to my editor Clare Rogers, who really brought this book together.

A special thank you to the members of our first home church—Chris F., Rick P., Morton and Lis H., Isabelle D.,

Nancy R., Christine G., Guy T., and others—who learned alongside me as we deepened our relationship with Jesus.

And, last but not least, without the support and encouragement of my wife, Amy, and our beautiful daughters, this book may never have seen the light of day. The doors that God has opened in my life are for you to walk through too. Bless you.

Endorsements

Hungry for an adventure with God? Then dive into the supernatural life and fulfill your desire for a deeper relationship with God as you get your own breakthrough into the supernatural realm. God wants to impart into your life a message of dramatic faith and empowerment as you encounter the risen Christ who is alive today! I've personally known Franklyn since 2005 and he's been a part of our ministry at Eagle Worldwide for many years. Grab a hold of this book, but more importantly grab a hold of the impartation to know God more deeply and intimately than ever before.

Apostle Russ Moyer
Founder and President of Eagle Worldwide Ministries
www.eagleworldwide.com

The testimony that Franklyn presents is that of one "who has put his hand to the plough" and not looked back. The journey has led him to the corners of the whited fields to harvest souls and make disciples. The Holy Spirit has gifted Franklyn with prophetic words that have spoken deeply into the hearts of those to whom he has ministered. Throughout the pages of this book, Franklyn provides keys to finding the oasis of God's presence in the situations in which we find ourselves in life. Journey with him as you learn to drink of the water of life, even in the dry places.

Dan Rosborough
Founder of Tent of David Ministries
www.tentofdavid.ca

Franklyn makes a bold choice in sharing some of his spiritual encounters with God in this refreshingly honest book. He reveals the reality of a God that we can and should still encounter even today. It is my privilege to recommend this book and can personally attest to his character as a sincere, radical believer in Christ!

Pastor René McIntyre
Founder and President of
Trumpet of Truth Christian Ministries
www.trumpetoftruth.org

Table of Contents

Introduction

There are a couple of reasons why this book has been written.

The first and most important reason is obedience to the Lord. When he asked me to share my supernatural experiences in writing I was daunted by this task, and yet I knew that this was a very clear directive. As a natural introvert, my first instinct was not to share my very private relationship and experiences with Jesus but, over time, I've come to realize that sharing my journey greatly benefits others. I'm thankful that the Lord has patience, since it's taken me around ten years to write this book!

The second reason for writing this book is to inspire you, the reader, to actively engage in your own adventure of faith with God.

This book is the beginning of my story. It is my testimony. Testimonies are the history of a person who has journeyed with God from wherever they started to a place where God has proven himself to be something to that person. For me,

God has proven himself to be amazing, surprising and a lot bigger than I had ever thought.

I firmly believe that everyone can have their own deep and rich relationship with Jesus. My prayer for you is that you will find my stories inspiring, and that they will challenge you to develop an even deeper relationship with him yourself.

Be blessed as you read this book.

Rev. Franklyn M. Spence

PART ONE

"Who are you, Lord?"

1.

The Audible Voice of God

---◆---

He who testifies to these things says,
"Yes, I am coming soon."
Amen. Come, Lord Jesus.

Revelation 22:20

***

I was utterly unprepared when it happened. But I guess you never can be prepared for hearing God's voice.

I was sixteen years old. I was walking across a playing field when I was stopped in my tracks by the sound of a voice speaking to me. The voice was God's. I don't mean that I had a feeling, or an idea, or a voice inside my head. I mean I heard, *with my ears,* God's voice speaking to me. It was as clear as someone standing right beside me.

This book is the story of how that summer day in 1987—and many like it over the years—have shaped my understanding of God and my relationship with him. It is my desire that as you read this story you'll grasp how much God longs to communicate with you too, in a unique and individual way.

The sound of his voice will change you in a moment. It will shake you to the very foundations of your existence and lift you to the highest mountain top, all in the blink of an eye. But one thing is clear—when you hear his voice, your life will never be the same. It can't be.

Sunday morning Christianity

Going to church throughout my childhood did nothing to prepare me for that moment in the middle of a playing field at a Christian summer camp. I was born in 1971 and grew up in the Baptist Church, first in Windsor and then in Mississauga, towns in southern Ontario, Canada. My parents and maternal grandparents were churchgoing folks, but faith was considered a private matter that was rarely discussed openly in our home. I don't ever remember praying together as a family, but we did say grace before meals (it was always said by my father and it was always the same words). My mother read her Bible regularly and my parents attended Bible studies on occasion. I have one older sister; growing up we never talked about our faith or deep spiritual topics. I guess you could say that my family were "Sunday morning Christians". I was a very shy teenager who loved to work on my own doing woodwork, art projects and drawing, and I was always the happiest doing activities where I could stay in the background.

Church was very predictable. Even before arriving at the building you knew exactly what would happen. We had three hymns out of the blue hymnal, and we always sang every verse of every song in its entirety. The pastor always spoke for twenty minutes, which seemed like a very long time, and my Dad often fell soundly asleep during the sermons. (This guaranteed him a firm jab in the ribs from my mother, especially when he suddenly started snoring, much to the delight of our fellow parishioners—but to the deep embarrassment of my sister and myself, who sank down low in our seats.)

The focus of the church I grew up in was Bible reading, Bible knowledge, and prayer, which provided a very solid theological approach to Christianity. The church didn't believe in miracles or healings or outwardly visible signs of the Holy Spirit. It's not that they were preaching against such things; it was more that they were a non-issue and never mentioned. I don't think anybody even considered asking God to intervene in anything, because it was just taken for granted that he was very distant; he had already given us everything we needed for contemporary life in the pages of scripture. God was very hands-off and far away. If I was to describe his main attitude towards us, it would be his hatred for sin.

So my idea of godliness was centered around daily scripture reading and quiet time with the Lord. My expectations were to gain scriptural knowledge and, if I were really blessed, to get some sort of "feeling" that God was with me.

I began reading scripture at a young age and by the time I was sixteen I had gotten to the book of Acts (having started with Genesis). This book came as a big surprise to me. I had the student edition of the Bible with some commentary at the beginning and throughout each book. The commentary said quite clearly that the book of Acts was about the "birth of the church". However, when I read it, it was nothing like my church experience at all. Acts was full of miracles and dramatic interventions by God. It was much more like an adventure story than a typical church service.

How on earth could this be the birth of the church? I had asked myself. And if it was, what happened to turn it into the church *I* knew? Why were these two things so radically different? Little did I know that God was preparing to respond to these questions in a dramatic way.

The voice in an empty field

While reading Acts and pondering those questions, I was working as a summer camp counselor at a Christian camp near Kingston, Ontario, in Canada. One afternoon I was taking my campers up to the main lodge across the playing field. The kids had run ahead of me, eager for the big game we were going to play, and I was alone in the middle of the field when I heard a voice.

It said:

"I am coming soon."

I literally stopped and turned around to see who had spoken to me. No one was there. The field was empty. Then at that moment the presence of the Holy Spirit hit me for the very first time in my life. The feeling was so overwhelming that I could only compare it to sticking your tongue into a light socket (which I've never done but don't recommend it!). Instantly all my systems were fried. I couldn't talk, couldn't think, couldn't do any-thing. I couldn't even put two thoughts together in my head, much less speak out a sentence.

There I was, smack in the middle of the impossible

The impossible had just happened! There was no doubt in my mind that God had clearly, without question, just spoken to me. Not as a thought or a feeling but as a sound! However, that was impossible because God never spoke to anyone any-more. Or even if he did, it would only be to a missionary in Africa—and then only in a life-or-death situation.

The only other people who "heard" from God, in my six-teen-year-old mind, were people who heard voices in their head due to mental illness, and I hoped I wasn't in that cat-egory. God just simply didn't do that anymore. Yet here I was caught in a paradox, and for about six hours afterwards I couldn't put two words together, couldn't think straight, had no idea what had just happened to me. My mind was spinning, my whole body vibrating with the echoes of those potent words . . .

"I am coming soon."

They were like hammer blows—not only to my mind, but to my body and spirit too.

Somehow I made it through the big game, dinner, and the after-dinner activities with dozens of people around me— no one questioned me, no one asked me anything, no one required anything of me. I did my duties as a camp counselor as if I was in a fog. The reverberations of those words hung in the air all around me.

I remember coming back to my senses back in my cabin on my bunk. My vision suddenly snapped back into focus. I had no idea how I got there, or what had happened in the intervening hours. By then it was after dark.

I was thinking, "What just happened to me?" and then, "Oh no—my campers!"

I'd been in such a state of shock, I didn't even know whether they'd gone to bed. I frantically went around to check each bed. They were all there, sound asleep—they were even in their pajamas. To this day I have no idea how that happened.

I was caught in a paradox. In the middle of an open field I had just stepped into the presence of a living God, but how could that be? I wasn't in a church service, I wasn't deep in worship; I was just in the middle of my day, going about my tasks, walking from my cabin to the main lodge. My theology didn't allow for this possibility. This was simply not possible.

Yet there I was, smack in the middle of the impossible.

Then I suddenly realized the actual words that had been spoken: "I am coming soon"—and I really started to panic. How soon is "soon"? Did he mean tonight? Was God coming tonight? Did he mean the *second coming*?

I'll tell you I was pretty scared. In fact, the whole "God episode" was very frightening, on top of being totally impossible. How could I resolve this inner conflict?

I needed to talk to someone, so later that evening, having emerged from my cabin more than a little shaken—I'm sure I must have been white as a ghost—I saw this friend of mine who was another camp counselor.

I sat with her and said, "I think God just spoke to me."

She looked at me weirdly.

"Um, okay…' she said. "What did he say?"

I told her, and again she looked at me very strangely. Then without saying anything she got up and left. She never mentioned it again. I felt rejected, and very quickly learned to keep my mouth shut after that. After all, I was a teenager who just wanted to fit in.

I was scared stiff; and I was caught in this no man's land theologically. God didn't speak to people anymore, and yet I was sure that I had heard his voice.

There seemed to be no answer to this paradox I was in. As a 16-year-old I was shy and deathly afraid of rejection, so I chose to just shut the whole "God episode" down. My choice was to move on, forget it. Perhaps I was suffering some sort of sunstroke or temporary weirdness or who knows what? Forget it, I thought, move on, let's get back to some sort of normal — or at least as 'normal' as sixteen can be.

Full-color, 3D encounter

A week or so later, still at the summer camp, I've succeeded in putting this "God episode" back into the farthest reaches of my mind. Then one day I'm walking towards the canoeing area to teach a canoeing class. Suddenly without any warning, everything around me disappears, and I'm caught up in an eyes-open, full-color, 3D encounter with God.

I see Jesus. He stretches out his hands wide and proclaims:

"This is how big I am!"

I know now that this experience is called an "open vision". Then, I feel like I've suddenly hit warp speed, and in a single instant I'm seeing the vastness of the whole universe. It's like grasping infinity in my hands.

I found myself lying on the ground trying to catch my breath. There were tears streaming down my face, and my head was spinning so fast I thought it was going to come right off. Words could not describe this feeling. The vastness of an endless, infinite God has just landed on my lap. No warning—nothing!

If I was confused before, I was even more confused now.

And why just then? Didn't God know I had a canoe class to teach?

Once again I couldn't speak, I couldn't think, and was utterly overwhelmed. Desperate to grasp onto something solid, all I knew is that I needed to get to the canoeing area to teach my class.

I honestly don't know how, but I got to the waterfront somehow, perhaps I had to crawl—I can't remember.

I do remember sitting on one of the logs thinking, "There is no way I can teach anything now. I can't think, I can't talk right. I'm really messed up."

However, none of the five campers that I was supposed to teach showed up for my class. No reason given. With all the people walking around no one spoke to me, not one word. After thirty minutes or so, I gave up waiting and went back to my room to try and pull together my life, which was clearly a shambles.

There was no explanation for this second "God episode". I was still stuck in an impasse between my understanding of who God is and what had just happened. My only recourse was to forget it, not think about it, ignore it and hope it will go away.

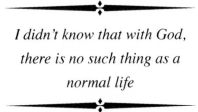

I didn't know that with God, there is no such thing as a normal life

Except that it didn't go away.

A week or so later I was in my room at camp reading scripture. I was about to go and help the rest of the staff clean out one of the buildings that was being used for storage. It was one of those everyone-meet-at-a-certain-place-and-time sort of thing. Five minutes before I need to go, the room around me disappears.

I look up and see Jesus again. This time he says:

"This is how much I love the world!"

God's love hits me like hurricane. It's like a spiritual earthquake, a physical force. My personal Richter scale is off the charts. I'm in tears—weeping, sobbing, unable to get off my bed. I can't even deal with my own sixteen-year-old emotions, let alone this spiritual tidal wave from outside of me!

But I'm also aware of the timing of this third "God episode".

"Why now? Why, if you really have to do this, and I wish you wouldn't because it's really messing me up, why now? Don't you know, God, I have to meet the rest of the staff right now?"

But as I lie there incapacitated, a weeping mess, caught up in a depth of emotion that is not my own and beyond my capacity to deal with by exponential amounts, there is a knock at my door.

One of the other staff pops his head in and announces, "Oh, the building is already cleared out, we've finished, and you don't need to come so you can have a few hours off. Bye."

And without so much as a glance at my clearly train-wrecked condition, I'm left mercifully alone to gather together the last few scraps of what I hoped was a normal life.

Of course I didn't know that with God, there is no such thing as a normal life.

2.

"Who are you, Lord?"

---◆---

For in him all things were created: things in heaven and on earth, visible and invisible, whether thrones or powers or rulers or authorities; all things have been created through him and for him. He is before all things, and in him all things hold together.

Colossians 1:16-17

***

It was a long time before I understood, or could even accept, what had hit me at that summer camp. The whole experience had seemed to come out of the blue, totally unbidden. But I now realize that, in a way, I had triggered it myself— by asking the Lord a question. For the first weeks of camp I had been reading the book of Acts. Puzzled by what I read, I had asked God an honest question: Why was my experience growing up in a traditional church so totally different than what I was reading in this book?

Acts reads like the script of a Hollywood blockbuster. There are narrow escapes, miraculous interventions, riots, and we see an explosive gospel that turned whole societies on their heads. It's spiritual dynamite. Up to that point in my life, I had only encountered a very different Jesus. One who was rather boring and very predictable. Where was this gospel that changed whole cities?

Without knowing it, my question had opened a door into the presence of God. To phrase this question in a different way, I was really asking: "Who are you, Lord?"

That was a far bigger and more dangerous question than I ever intended to ask.

Who are you, Lord?

At that summer camp Jesus began to answer my question, and my "Sunday morning Christianity" was

That was a far bigger and more dangerous question than I ever intended to ask

blown out of the water. He gave me three answers: "I am coming soon"; "This is how big I am"; and "This is how much I love the world".

Is God distant, remote, disinterested? No! *I am coming soon.* Jesus is near. He is closely involved with us in spirit, and any day now he will physically stand among us again.

29

Is God irrelevant (except on a Sunday morning)? No! *This is how big I am.* He is infinite and eternal. He encompasses the whole universe; every atom of it was created through him and for him, and "...in him all things hold together" (Col 1:17).

Is God's main attitude towards us "hatred of sin"? No! *This is how much I love the world.* His main attitude towards us is love, a love of such huge dimensions that it's way beyond our ability to grasp. God *is* love (1 John 4:16).

No one could be less boring or predictable than this Jesus I had just encountered.

Even now over 25 years later I'm still unpacking these statements. I ponder these three answers on a regular basis and continue to find new meaning in them. There is so much of God's identity tied up in them, almost as if he's presented them as his personal mission statement—and in a way, mine too. That his return is imminent, that he is bigger than anyone or any problem, and that his love knows no limits.

His answers still take my breath away.

Do you dare to ask?

But I'm not the first person to ask, "Who are you, Lord?" There was a very angry man named Saul who asked it first:

> ...Saul was still breathing out murderous threats against the Lord's disciples. He went to the high priest and asked him for letters to the synagogues in Damascus, so that if he found

any there who belonged to the Way, whether
men or women, he might take them as pris-
oners to Jerusalem. As he neared Damascus
on his journey, suddenly a light from heaven
flashed around him. He fell to the ground and
heard a voice say to him, "Saul, Saul, why do
you persecute me?"

"Who are you, Lord?" Saul asked.

"I am Jesus, whom you are persecuting," he
replied. "Now get up and go into the city, and
you will be told what you must do."

Acts 9:1-6

Saul's life was completely and utterly turned upside down.
He went from a man who was actively seeking the murder of
Christians to becoming the apostle of grace to the Gentiles.

The answers I received—and continue to receive—turned
my life upside down too. When God shows you who he
is, you cannot go away
unchanged. The mere act
of revealing himself will
challenge your unbelief,
reveal your destiny, and
show you his character all at the same time.

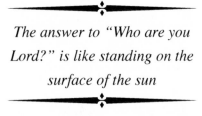

The answer to "Who are you Lord?" is like standing on the surface of the sun

The answer to that question isn't just in words, since
mere words can never hope to describe God—you have to

experience him. And when God answers by revealing who he is to you, you cannot come away unchanged. You'll have to respond with some pretty big changes in your life. There is no way that you can't respond. The sheer vastness of God will humble you, his love will roll over you like an ocean wave, his sacrifice will shake you to the very foundations of your soul.

The answer to "Who are you Lord?" is like standing on the surface of the sun. That is his nature. You will be utterly transformed.

3.

The Girl with the Injured Hands

---

*Now may the God of peace, who through the blood of the
eternal covenant brought back from the dead our Lord
Jesus, that great Shepherd of the sheep, equip you with
everything good for doing his will, and may he work in us
what is pleasing to him, through Jesus Christ, to whom be
glory for ever and ever. Amen.*

Hebrews 13:20

***

When I went home at the end of that summer camp, I
was still very much stuck in this paradox between the
God of my understanding and what I had just experienced. I
told myself that camp is a special place—but now it's back
to reality. Since I was quite shy, and knew absolutely nothing
about how the Holy Spirit works, I decided to say nothing to

33

anyone about these "God episodes". My strategy was to keep quiet and hope it would go away. Maybe it was just a phase I was going through?

In discussions about God at my church youth group, nobody described anything like what I'd experienced, not even remotely. The audible voice of God? Are you serious? Only strange people hear from God. So I tried to forget about all the spiritual stuff going on in my life, and I busied myself with being a normal teenager.

I was not "Pentecostal"; I didn't know anything about the Holy Spirit, and I had never heard of any miracles happening nowadays. I had never heard of anyone who had even heard of anyone who had actually experienced a direct miracle. In fact, at church nothing like this was ever mentioned — if it was something that we ever thought about. I remember discussions with some of the forward-thinking adults of the church who were contemplating raising their hands during worship. This was considered quite radical. Our church didn't do any "ministry time" (praying with individual church members as part of the service or after the service), or "testimonies" of how they had found faith (that I heard anyway), and your level of faith was strictly governed by how often you attended church. At least that was my impression as a teenager. A good Christian had regular church attendance, and backslidden believers only came at Christmas and Easter.

But I'd just had what I would now call a series of open visions and spiritual encounters with the Lord, each more powerful than the last. (At that time I had no idea what they were, or even the language to describe them.) These events were a profound mystery to me—a mystery I was eager to forget so I could get along with living my teenage life.

"You have the gift of prophecy"

At this time, I was in a great youth group at a Baptist church in Mississauga, Ontario. One long weekend the following spring, we all attended a huge youth conference with about six hundred other youth from across Ontario. It was probably the first real conference I had been to. I was excited to go, as we were told there was going to be a huge water fight and some top Christian bands performing.

On the second day of the conference after the evening meeting, just as I was leaving the big hall, the Lord spoke to me again. This time he told me, in no uncertain terms, to go to the conference speaker and explain to her what had been happening to me.

This experience had left me just as shaken up as the ones at the summer camp; the tears were streaming down my face and I was shaking like a leaf. I found the speaker in another building, and we sat down on the floor. Somehow, I was able to tell her what had been happening. The words spilled out of me like a dam that had burst.

She listened very politely and then said, "Oh, is that all? You have the gift of prophecy."

Then she immediately stood up and walked out of the room. No explanation, no nothing, not another word—she just walked away leaving me sitting on floor.

"The gift of what?... What is this? Hey, don't just leave me here, the gift of what??? What are you talking about? Don't just leave me here..."

But she was gone.

I sat there on the floor for a while, and then I remember walking out of the room in a fog, totally stunned. I went over to a picnic table and sat down. I had no idea what was happening to me, but at that moment a strange peace settled over me.

Then for the first time, I got what I now know as the "still small voice of the Lord"; not an audible voice, but a quiet voice inside my own heart. It said, "Well, son. Now you have a name for it, are you going to accept this gift or not?"

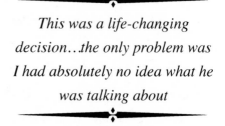

This was a life-changing decision...the only problem was I had absolutely no idea what he was talking about

There was a real sense that this was a life-changing moment, a crossroads, and decision that would affect the rest of my life.

The only problem was I had absolutely no idea what he was talking about.

Prophecy? What was that? It was only a name. I remember reading 1 Corinthians, where it's mentioned, but that was it. I had never heard a single teaching session on this topic, read no books about it, and never heard of anyone having any sort of "spiritual gift" at all. Truly, I had no clue. The conference speaker might as well have been speaking a different language. As far as I was concerned, prophecy was for the Old Testament.

So I said to the still small voice of the Lord, "Let me sleep on it. I'll tell you in the morning."

After a rather sleepless night I woke up with a very tiny glimmer of faith. Something had occurred to me about perspective.

It went like this: the perspective on our own life is like walking along the bottom of a wooded valley — we can't see very far ahead, and we don't have much of a long-distance view. We can only see what is directly around us. But God's perspective is from the mountain top, and he has the long-distance view. He can see what is up the valley ahead of us.

So if he thinks the gift of prophecy is a good idea, whatever that actually means, then I guess it's okay by me . . . I think . . . maybe.

That was my big statement of faith. About two hours later, it received its first test.

Take the bandages off

The day before, in a food line-up during lunch, I'd met this girl whose both hands were all bandaged up with finger splints. I asked her what had happened, and it turned out she had been playing volleyball and dived for the ball, landed on her hands wrong, and the rest is history. I never got her name.

This was the final day of the conference and we were heading into the last meeting before we all went home. I was sitting there minding my own business with my whole youth group of about thirty kids, most of whom went to my high school, all on the same bench.

During the sermon God spoke to me again and said, "Look to your left."

I look over and the same girl I had met with the bandaged fingers was sitting on a bench against the wall. She was sobbing, and a friend of hers was holding her. She was really crying her eyes out.

God said to me, "Give your books to the person beside you, stand up, go over to her and pray for her. Tell her she's healed, take the bandages off her hands and come back and sit down. I'll heal her hands, but more importantly I'll heal her heart."

As a sixteen-year-old, non-charismatic Baptist kid who has never prayed for anything serious, never seen the pastors do anything more than your basic blessing prayer, never even heard of a modern miracle, and is pretty sure that they no longer happened (at least in North America), this request was like hitting the panic button.

So I convinced myself that there was no way that this "voice" could be God. Why would God make me this uncomfortable, push me out of my comfort zone, especially in front of my whole youth group? I was paralyzed with fear. Tell her she's healed *and* take the bandages off!

"Forget it," was my response. "There is no way I'm doing that! Besides what would I even say?"

So he told me what to say. I can't remember exactly what it was—I probably wasn't even listening at the time. I only remember it was a very basic prayer.

"No," I said, "I won't do it. Anyway, how do I even know that this is God? Demons disguise themselves as angels of light, you know. You have to test the spirits."

(I had no idea what that meant but I remembered reading it somewhere.)

So I think to myself, how do I "test the spirits?" The only thing I could think of was to randomly open my Bible and point to any verse, and if it relates then I know it's God.

So I did that, randomly flipped my Bible open and stuck my finger down on a verse. This is what I got:

> Now may the God of peace, who through the blood of the eternal covenant brought back from the dead our Lord Jesus, that great Shepherd of the sheep, equip you with every-thing good for doing his will, and may he work in us what is pleasing to him, through Jesus Christ, to whom be glory for ever and ever. Amen.
>
> Hebrews 13:20-21

This verse was like an arrow through my heart.

"Are you kidding me?" I said in my heart. "Equip you with everything good for doing his will? Work in us what is pleasing to him? That's not very funny."

My "testing the spirits" was supposed to be my excuse to get out of this, but instead I found myself in a deeper faith crisis.

On and on I went, justifying my unbelief, and why I couldn't possibly go over and pray for this girl and actually remove the finger splints and bandages. That he should just pick someone more qualified, pick the speaker or one of the youth leaders or, for that matter, anybody except me.

Why me?

Then the preacher finished her message and we all stood up to sing a song.

I've never sung this song before, or since, but it will forever be burned into my brain. The title was *When Jesus Calls, I Will Answer Yes*.

I couldn't even mouth the words. When Jesus calls I will answer yes! The weight of the world was on my shoulders. I was in a full-blown faith crisis.

It was literally only two hours since I had reluctantly agreed to go ahead with God's mystery plan for my life. It felt like time had slowed down. That was the longest hymn I never sang. It was sheer agony. I felt that I was going to sweat blood. I was in panic mode! I didn't know anybody who knew anybody who'd even *heard* of anybody who'd had a real miracle, and somehow I was being expected to do this? Me? Why me?

In the space of less than twelve hours, I'd been confronted with the audible voice of God again, revealed my very, very secret spiritual events to another person, made a life-changing decision, had a sleepless night, accepted the reality of spiritual gifts which I knew nothing about, and now I was being asked to walk over to a total stranger who is obviously in distress (a girl, no less) and perform a double miracle.

Let me tell you, if I had an ejector seat right then, I would have been pulling that rip cord to escape.

While I was busy arguing with God, the song was ending. Little did the organizer know that someone in the audience would have to take this song so literally. As it happened, Jesus *was* calling me personally and my answer certainly was *not* yes. My answer was, "No way!"

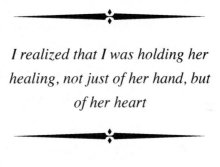

I realized that I was holding her healing, not just of her hand, but of her heart

It was at this moment that I realized something: we weren't singing just any song, we were singing the *closing song*, meaning this was the end of the meeting. It was the last event of the whole conference.

This was it, there were no more chances left. No more time for arguing with God, do it or don't do it—this was it.

41

That was the point I realized that I was holding her healing, not just of her hand, but of her heart. I was holding her healing in *my* very own hands. God had entrusted that to me, and what was I doing? Wasting time arguing!

I realized that for whatever reason God wasn't going to walk over there and do it himself, he wasn't going to send someone more experienced or, for that matter, more willing. He had entrusted her healing to me, and this was a time-limited offer. I had quite literally run out of time.

Now the song had finished, everyone was starting to leave, and the panic that was in my heart fled only to be replaced by a different panic. If I don't do this now, this instant, then the moment will be gone never to return again.

She is standing up to leave, still crying. Quickly I hand my books to my friend beside me, literally tossing them in his lap, and struggle to get from the middle of the row to the aisle.

Now all 600 people from the conference are in the aisles trying to leave, chatting to each other. The aisles are choked full of people, you can barely move, and she has left first. I'm fighting to make up ground, to catch up with her—there's thirty people ahead of me, now twenty, then ten, and just at the barn doors I'm right behind her, and as I'm reaching out to grab her shoulder, for some reason, I freeze.

I stand there, frozen, with my arm stretched out in mid-air, having come to within one inch of stopping her and I've blocked up, choked up, and frozen.

All the other people are filing past me, hundreds of teenagers and my whole youth group, as I stand there in the middle of the doorway my arm still outstretched frozen in mid-air. I watch her walk away without looking back, never knowing that God has heard her cry. Fear had stopped me; the fear in a young man's heart had stifled the work of the Holy Spirit.

4.

Failing my First Test

The Spirit searches all things, even the deep things of God.

1 Corinthians 2:10b

***

This wasn't how I imagined Christianity to be.

I remember sermons preached at our church about people like Jonah and the apostles— how they had run away from God or struggled to believe—and I had unknowingly judged them, thinking, "Those idiots! If I ever had the word of the Lord I would certainly know what to do."

Yet there I was, standing in the middle of the doorway, 600 kids filing past me, with my arm outstretched in mid-air, with not only the word of the Lord, but a scripture and a song to confirm it too, and somehow I couldn't pull myself together to deliver the message.

Where was my brash youthful confidence now? Somehow all those hymns and uplifting sermons weren't helping at this point. Sunday school classes and all those cartoon strips we had been given as kids with the Old Testament stories had not prepared me in any way whatsoever for this moment.

I had let God down, I had let myself down, and most certainly I had let this girl down. Up to that moment I really thought I was a good Baptist kid. After all, I read my Bible, prayed a lot and attended services regularly. Somehow I had assumed that this meant I was mature in my faith, at least for my age.

Yet here I was. God had given me clear, unquestionable step-by-step instructions, backed up by scripture and independently confirmed by a hymn, but in that crucial moment I had choked up and frozen. As a result, not only did that young lady not

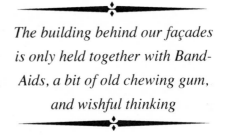

The building behind our façades is only held together with Band-Aids, a bit of old chewing gum, and wishful thinking

receive her healing but she didn't get to know that God had heard her. She didn't get to know that God cared for her heart as well as her hand.

I had let the team down.

It took many years before I realized that God's plans are not thwarted by one person's lack of obedience. He knew he was pushing me well past my abilities. He was doing that on purpose, not so that a person would be robbed of their healing but to reveal to me the state of my own heart.

My pride in being Baptist, of thinking I had it all together, of knowing what God and Christianity is all about ... ha! What did I know? One simple request from God, just for a prayer and a statement of faith, and my whole world crumbled to dust and ashes.

I now know that God has a way of obliterating our facades that we erect to show the world how great we are, with just one or two sentences. And the truth is that the building behind the façade is only held together with Band-Aids, a bit of old chewing gum, and wishful thinking.

The truth of seeing yourself how you really, really are hurts. Anyone who tells you differently is a liar. It's very difficult to see yourself as you really are. When you've put up a mask or a façade without even realizing it, it will hurt when it's removed. But in the end, it's the truth that sets you free (John 8:32).

Arguing with God

That girl walked away, never knowing that God cared about her problems.

Now I wonder, how many thousands upon thousands of times has that happened? How many times has God asked someone to do something little for him and we start arguing? And we argue and complain for long enough that the moment passes, the window of opportunity shuts, and the burden of obedience gets passed onto someone else. How many times have you done that?

But let's put the shoe on the other foot. If that girl were you, and you needed a touch from God—a healing for your hand and a healing in your heart—if that was you, I think you would appreciate it if the person who got the assignment for your healing got over all their petty issues and got on with the business of doing the work of God's kingdom.

God wanted to show mercy to this young woman. He wanted to show that he had heard her cry. He wanted to show that he is a healer,

One of the best things that can happen to you is to totally fail God's tests

physically and emotionally, but I was too concerned about my perception of justice. I felt it wasn't fair for God to ask me to do something I felt uncomfortable doing, something that stretched me or took me out of my comfort zone. Christianity was all about staying firmly in the middle of my comfort zone. Everyone knew that. Everyone apparently, except God.

My sense of justice was all about what I felt was fair to me, but God's heart was moved by something else completely. His heart was moved by compassion for whatever this young girl was going through. God wanted to show mercy, but I was interested in protecting my dignity and hiding in my unbelief.

It is very scary when God starts digging into the soil of our hearts. It doesn't take him long to find the roots of many weeds that we would be happier to deny even existed. One thing I couldn't deny was that God had given me a test, a test that I had clearly failed. But I've since learned that one of the best things that can happen to you is to totally fail God's tests.

When you blow it, but you realize that God was testing and you totally screwed up, that's a good place to be. Failure is a great teacher if you are willing to listen. God does not set you up for failure—he sets you up for success. He gives us tests so that we can pass them, but when we do fail God will use our failure to teach us. Our failures in spiritual tests are the best revealers of the true condition of our heart.

This is a great blessing, even if it doesn't feel like it. In fact, it usually hurts a lot!

Learning that your heart isn't actually in the place you thought it was is the first step to real, authentic spiritual growth. We are very good at unknowingly lying to ourselves, especially about our spiritual condition. It takes these tests to really show us where we truly are.

We can listen to good sermons and read good books, and because this information has come across our path we tell ourselves that we have grown spiritually to the level of the messages we've heard or read.

But it takes the passing or failing of God's tests to truly show us where our hearts and our faith are really at. It's one thing to be sitting in a pew and to tell yourself that you have strong faith, but the pew isn't the test. It's when you're in the trenches that you find out what you're made of.

It may sound crazy—but be thankful for the tests you receive. How you react in the test is the only true measure of where you are really at in your spiritual walk.

When you pass the test, be grateful and give God your praise; and when you fail, remember, you will learn a hundred times more from your failures than you will from your successes. That failure, even though it hurts, can be used by the Holy Spirit to minister to you—if you let God use it in the way he meant. When you realize that, you can praise him in the failure too.

God knows when you will mess it up. He doesn't place these obstacles in your path so that you fall or beat yourself up; but he uses them as a catalyst for your growth.

This growth will happen if you allow the Holy Spirit to be who he is—your counselor.

5.

The Choice

---◆◆---

Are not two sparrows sold for a penny? Yet not one of them
will fall to the ground outside your Father's care.

Matthew 10:29

***

The youth conference and my failure at this first spiritual test was followed, a few months later, by the next summer vacation. This summer I worked as a camp counselor at a different Christian summer camp near Bracebridge, Ontario, Canada.

A bird with a broken neck

At the junior campsite there is a meeting hall at the top of a hill overlooking Lake Clearwater. It was called the Crow's Nest, and it featured a whole wall of windows with a balcony showcasing the exceptional view of the lake. I used to go up to this building to do my daily quiet time with the Lord where I would read scripture and pray.

One day I remember I just couldn't concentrate. I tried reading scripture and the words blurred on the page; I tried to pray and I couldn't think of anything to say. So I decided to get some air out on the balcony. After a few minutes of looking out onto the lake but still getting nowhere, I turned to leave, and as I did so there was a huge bang right next to my head. I nearly jumped out of my skin. I had no idea what had happened, but looking around I saw a sparrow lying on the floor next to my feet.

It had flown into the window at full speed just as I had turned away. I didn't even see it coming. The sparrow was lying on the floor of the balcony, at the base of the windows, still alive but obviously severely injured. Its head was bent at an unnatural angle, its eyes glazed and half shut. It was twitching and, most distressingly, making these little sad peeping noises.

"Oh no," I thought, "What do I do?"

I was really upset. I needed to do something, and quick, to try to save this little bird's life. My first thought was I could take the bird to the camp nurse—she'd know what to do.

Then I thought, "That's a dumb idea. She's a nurse, not a vet."

I was also a bit concerned about being pecked.

What do I do? . . . What do I do? . . .

I'm pacing back and forth, up and down the balcony, and the sparrow is making these sad little sounds and continuing to twitch in a most distressing way. It was clearly suffering from a broken neck.

What do I do? . . . What do I do?

I'm thinking, "I can't leave it suffering like this. Maybe I should help it along to its final 'destination' (so to speak) but I'm not sure I could do that either."

I'm panicking a bit.

What do I do? . . . What do I do?

Undecided, I go back inside the building, sit down and rather flippantly say, "OK God, what do you expect me to do about this?"

I really wasn't expecting any sort of answer. People say this kind of thing to God all the time and never get an answer. It's a rhetorical question. The whole point of a rhetorical question is that you're not supposed to get an answer. However, this time was different.

"Stand up, go outside and heal the bird."

That was the answer I got. Clear as day.

Not the answer I was expecting, if any.

"What!? Heal the bird? Whoa, wait a minute now . . . We've been through this before with that girl at the conference. I can't do that. Remember what happened last time?"

"Stand up, go outside and heal the bird."

An invisible battle

Suddenly I felt pinned to my seat, like a great weight was pressing down on me. It was a moment of spiritual battle. Had I been able to see into the spirit, I'm sure whole armies were battling it out right in front of me.

This was one of those focusing experiences, where the whole world disappears around you and your whole life comes down to one decision. But I was still arguing.

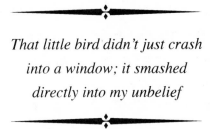

That little bird didn't just crash into a window; it smashed directly into my unbelief

I said, "God we've been through this before with the girl and her hand."

"Stand up . . .
go outside . . .
and heal the bird."

Again I found myself in a crisis of faith. Within one minute I'd gone from quitting my unproductive prayer time, to full-blown panic, to a pivot point in my spiritual journey.

This was the sort of crazy moment that's only supposed to happen in a Hollywood movie. This was the moment of deciding whose side I'm really on.

Does God exist to serve my needs, or am I here to serve his?

The spiritual battle raged on around me.

53

Every church I had ever attended believed the same thing about miracles, that God had finished with all that. All the miracles that were ever going to happen had already been done. If you needed a healing, then get up and go to the doctor.

When I said I felt pinned to my seat, I was literally pinned to my seat. I couldn't move. But I knew I needed to choose, and this was a choice that I had never expected to have to take. After all, Baptists never have faith crises! We are far too predictable for that; nothing ever rocks the boat.

"Stand up . . .

go outside . . .

and heal the bird."

The words hung in the air like thunderclaps.

Who ever thought a sparrow could cause such havoc? That little bird didn't just crash into a window; it smashed directly into my unbelief.

But in that moment I made my choice, an irrevocable choice.

I chose God over my unbelief.

I chose God over the security of anonymity.

I chose God over the predictability and stability of my Baptist background.

I chose faith.

Literally one arm at a time—like some scrawny wannabe superhero facing my kryptonite moment—I wrestled my left arm free, then my right. The hardest thing in my whole life, the absolute hardest thing I've ever, ever had to do, was to raise myself up off that seat.

This was an act of will. It was harder than climbing a mountain. It took not only every muscle but every ounce of sheer will I had.

My choice had to come into direct conflict with all the forces of darkness arrayed against me at that moment. My choice had come into direct conflict with my spiritual upbringing. My choice had come into direct conflict with my shy, introverted personality.

To choose faith, to choose action, to advance in the face of the unknown: I had made my decision and now I must act. I had chosen faith over fear. What I didn't realize at the time was that fear had been controlling me, sucking the faith out of me like a spiritual leech. That was why I had failed my first test.

Then, having wrestled myself upright to free my left foot, one staggering step, then my right—and slowly but surely I made the short crossing to the door of the balcony, each step faster and easier than the last. Then I was outside.

The sparrow was still there, still twitching and peeping, its eyes glazed over. It was in its last moment of life.

Quickly, before my courage failed me, I knelt down beside the bird, and then I had this sinking realization: I don't know what to say.

No, I really didn't know what to say. All those church Sunday school classes on Noah's ark weren't helping me at this moment. Was there some special formula, some sort of secret prayer that only a few know?

What do you say when kneeling on a balcony beside a dying sparrow with a broken neck?

Where are my three hymns and nice uplifting message now? Everything I ever knew about Christianity fled from me at that moment. I've got nothing, zero, zip, I'm a complete blank.

Then the tiniest of lifelines appeared, like a faint wisp of smoke. I had a vague memory of a scripture or perhaps a song, I couldn't be sure, that said, "There is power in the name of Jesus." I didn't know what that meant, or what kind of power, but I was desperate for anything.

So in a shaky voice I spoke out loud, somewhere between a squeak and a whisper: "In Jesus' name be healed."

The words barely trickled out of my mouth. It felt like they were running down my chin and falling to the floor.

Nothing happened. What! After all this? Nothing? Well, perhaps God didn't hear me.

I straightened myself up, took a deep breath, and this time with a bit more force and perhaps I even got above a whisper, this time I spoke it again.

"In Jesus' name be healed."

It was at that moment my life changed as much as the sparrow's. Right in front of my eyes, that little broken bird's shoulder popped back into place. Right in front of my eyes, without touching it, it just popped back into place. Its head, which had been flattened on one side popped back out like an inflatable ball bouncing back into shape. Its neck, which had been at an unnatural angle, straightened out. It blinked, and the eyes that had been glazed over instantly cleared. It jumped up off the floor onto its feet and started singing a beautiful song, right there, right in front of me! It was healed!

A miracle right in front of my eyes!

It kept singing and singing the most beautiful song, and I believe it was praising the Lord! In fact, while I was speechless, it had regained its voice very well and knew exactly what to say. With all its little voice it praised the Lord.

Facing the living God

I, on the other hand, was in shock. The creative, miraculous power of God had just stepped out of the past and into the present. God had stepped out of the pages of scripture, where my "comfort zone" kept him mummified deep in the annals of the past, into a very present reality.

I had to come to terms with a God who had his own voice and his own will, separate from my own, who had made his choice to intervene in the here and now.

I had been sheltered by this sense of time, that God only did things in the past; the far distant past. That was a God you could control. A God of long ago is a God that you can take in small portions, here and there as you feel like it.

Moses and Jonah and many other characters in scripture all had to deal with their own faith crises. It's comforting to read about their lives, and pick some uplifting passage that will stroke your ruffled feathers but not actually confront you. When you read about them and their issues, you can laugh and feel better about yourself and tell yourself that you'd surely do much better if you were in their shoes.

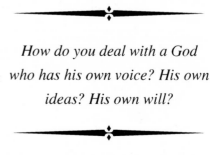

How do you deal with a God who has his own voice? His own ideas? His own will?

But when it's *you* standing at the shores of your Red Sea, with only a staff in your hands, all the Israelites looking at you and Pharaoh's army bearing down on you to slaughter your entire nation, it's a different story altogether.

This was a God who clearly wasn't playing by my rule book, and wasn't listening to my logic or excuses. He was going—and quite deliberately I might add—outside the box, coloring outside of the lines, skiing off-piste.

How do you deal with a God who has his own voice? His own ideas? His own will? This was the uncharted territory of the risen Lord.

This was raw relationship, where all the formalities and niceties of a pleasant church service vanish in a tsunami of the presence of a Living God. This God was wild at heart and up for adventure—and my faith had to do some catching up.

He was ready to climb mountains and forge rivers, whereas I was struggling to get off the couch.

I was now clearly embarked on a journey, a difficult, steep path to confront and overcome my inner Pharisee and step into a place of faith. The *Away in a Manger* baby Jesus had now been replaced by a white-water rafting Jesus who'd decided that we were going on a little trip—to points unknown. And I was coming with him.

> Are not two sparrows sold for a penny? Yet
> not one of them will fall to the ground outside
> your Father's care.

> Matthew 10:29

In a way there were two sparrows that day, just as in that scripture—one literal, one metaphorical—but both had an encounter. One got healed but the other one, namely me, got set free. I had to stare down my fear and unbelief. I had to make a choice. Choose the safety of the known, or choose the adventure of the unknown? Choose fear, or choose faith? I chose faith, and in doing so, chose the unknown with God.

What happened to that little bird? Well, by the time the healing had happened, the bell had long since rung for breakfast—so I had to leave him there singing the praises of the Lord. After the meal, as soon as I had a moment I rushed back. By that time, he had gone; flown away, free at last.

6.

Uniquely Unqualified

… I pray that you, being rooted and established in love,
may have power, together with all the Lord's holy people,
to grasp how wide and long and high and deep is the
love of Christ, and to know this love that surpasses
knowledge—that you may be filled to the measure of all the
fullness of God.

Ephesians 3:17-19

***

This was my introduction to Christian life. I was launched, somewhat unwillingly, into some sort of calling; although whatever it was I had no idea.

I was the worst sort of recruit.

It's not about me

If you think about the personal qualities one would associate with this calling, I'm sure I had none of them—I was shy and far more interested in spending time alone working on my projects for art college than approaching strangers or rocking the boat. However, personal characteristics aside, I had made my choice when I said "yes" to him.

When I think of the heroes of scripture, certain traits come to mind. To me, they were strong-willed people who never took the easy road. They were people who didn't shy away from interpersonal conflict. They had no qualms about walking up to kings and commoners alike and telling them plainly all their sins even when this put them in harm's way. They were strong and not intimidated by any man-made authority. These were leaders, immensely confident and charismatic. Some were so independent of any man-made system that they lived in the desert, eating wild bugs and honey.

I wasn't sure what wild bugs taste like but I was pretty sure I wouldn't like them.

What did I have in common with any of these? I had far too much Jonah in me and far too little Apostle Paul. I didn't like conflict and hated dealing with issues directly. Although I could force myself to talk in front of groups it was a tiring process that I worried and fretted about for weeks beforehand.

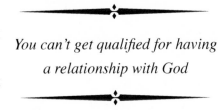

You can't get qualified for having a relationship with God

You could say I was uniquely unqualified for this—whatever "this" was.

It wasn't until years later that I discovered that my total lack of abilities is standard with God. God rarely picks "qualified" people; if he did, they would be able to accomplish his plan in their own strength and abilities. No, he picks the most unqualified people who are willing to enter into a journey with him.

The secret is that it's not about you. It's really, really not about you. It's always, always about him.

So God doesn't look to your abilities for the accomplishment of his will—he looks to his own abilities.

In reality there aren't any qualified people. You can't get qualified for having a relationship with God. You can only go from unwilling to willing, to actively engaging in faith. So whatever God has called you to do, don't worry about being qualified. Was David "qualified" to conquer Goliath? At the first reading of this popular Bible story it certainly seems to be an uneven fight. But the Bible is full of "impossible" situations. God always calls people to the impossible. The completely, totally impossible. This is normal for him. That way he gets to have the fun of showing us how amazing and how powerful he truly is, and we can then praise him for it and honestly say—it's not me, it's him.

From believing to knowing

Everyone's journey with God will be different.

After the sparrow-healing incident, I entered into a long season of dialogue with God. How I wish I had known the importance of writing everything down—those early experiences were not recorded. What I do remember is that I would be reading scripture, and I would get a running commentary from the Lord during it. I would get explanations and his feelings. Answers to my questions were often immediate and very deep.

This was the beginning of our relationship. Jesus was becoming my friend; someone I could talk to.

I was slowly discovering what a difference there is between relationship and religion. Unknowingly, I had only experienced religion up to this point: it was an event that you attended on a Sunday morning. Relationship is 24/7. It's with you all the time.

Faith starts you on the journey. At the beginning of that journey you can say, "I *believe* that God is faithful"; but by the time you reach your destination you'll be able to say, "I *know* that God is faithful." The difference

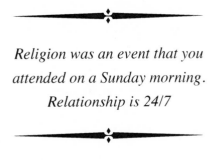

Religion was an event that you attended on a Sunday morning. Relationship is 24/7

between believing and knowing is the journey of faith. Faith will have accomplished its mission when your testimony changes from "I believe" to "I know."

It's like the force of gravity. Although I can't see gravity, I know that when I wake up tomorrow morning I won't float out of bed. Gravity doesn't need to prove itself to me—it's just a fact. It's the same with the journey of faith. When its process is complete, then God won't have to prove his faithfulness to you—it will simply be a fact, because you've experienced it.

7.

The Creative Voice of God

---◆---

*But if an unbeliever or an inquirer comes in while everyone
is prophesying, they are convicted of sin and are brought
under judgment by all, as the secrets of their hearts are laid
bare. So they will fall down and worship God, exclaiming,
"God is really among you!"*

1 Corinthians 14:24-25

***

By the time I was in my early twenties, I was well and truly
embarked on the adventure of hearing God's voice—and
learning to obey him, even when I didn't fully understand.
This chapter tells one story that taught me both the importance of trusting and obeying him, and the incredibly unique
and creative ways he finds to speak to us.

A wooden sculpture

After I graduated from high school, I started a four-year program in sculpture/installation at the prestigious Ontario College of Art and Design (OCAD) in Toronto, Ontario. I wanted to be a professional sculptor and have a glossy coffee-table book of my work published before I was 30 years old—that was my big dream!

While I was in Toronto I joined a Christian art group called AIR Waves ("Artists In Revival"). This unique group was led by an artist named Rick Berry, and it held events that were both performance art and free-flowing ministry in the Spirit. They fully embraced the gifts of the Spirit, and they were like no other Christian meeting I had ever experienced before; it was very exciting to be a part of. This was a far cry from the church of my childhood!

One morning, just as I was waking up, the Lord spoke to me.

He said, "I want you to make something for me."

He gave me a picture in my head of a wooden container or sculpture. It was long and pointy at both ends and made on a wood lathe. There were two equal parts to this container, and at the join in the middle, there was writing. On one side of the container was a list of the names of God, and on the other side a list of spiritual gifts. Inside the container I was shown to put red rose petals—but I was also told to add a very specific scent that he would show me later.

The whole picture of this unusual sculpture landed right in my mind in one shot, just like getting handed a set of blueprints.

"OK Lord," I said. "I can make that for you."

I had no idea what the container was about or what it was for, but because he'd asked me to make it I was happy to do it. He had been very specific about what

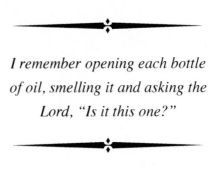

I remember opening each bottle of oil, smelling it and asking the Lord, "Is it this one?"

he wanted, so I had to do my best to be as accurate and faithful to the vision as I could be. I got to work. It took a few weeks to make it, and the trickiest part was finding the correct scent for the rose petals.

He had shown me that he wanted a specific scent, but I didn't know what it was. So I went down to a store that sold special shampoos and soaps where they had a whole rack of scented oils. I remember standing in front of this rack opening each bottle of oil, smelling it and asking the Lord, "Is it this one?"

"No," he said to the first one.

"How about this one?"

"No."

"This?"

"No."

"How about this one?"

No, no, no, no...

And on and on this went for ages, until about thirty minutes later, I finally got a "Yes".

When I had finished the wooden container, I still did not know what it was for or what the Lord wanted me to do with it. I had simply made it out of obedience.

Then one day he told me, "Take the container to the next AIR Waves meeting."

"Ok, Lord."

So I brought the wooden container to the artists' meeting, and I told the group that I didn't really know what it was for, or even what it was, but the Lord specifically told me to make it by giving me the blueprints and told me to bring it to this meeting.

God speaks—through a scent

A member of the group who was a modern dancer gently took the container out of my hands and started doing a spontaneous worship dance. A musician began to play, and it turned into a wonderful worship experience. At one point the dancer opened the container and started sprinkling the rose petals over people.

When he got to a woman who had never come to our meeting before, as the petals landed on her she started to cry, then to sob, and then it became that kind of deep, uncontrollable sobbing where she had to take deep gasps of breath.

Then she fell off her chair onto the floor, weeping and weeping for a long time.

I hadn't been sure what to expect from this sculpture, but I really wasn't expecting this. I'm sure everyone was touched by the dance and the artwork, but this woman was clearly deeply affected beyond anyone else, and nobody knew who she was or why she was so moved. We didn't know her name or anything about her as we had never met her before.

Afterwards I went to her to find out what had happened to her during the worship.

She slowly explained to me that her faith had been on very rocky ground for a long time, and that she wasn't sure if God was real, or even if she believed in him anymore.

Then about two weeks before this meeting, her husband had told her that he didn't love her anymore and he wanted a divorce. She was totally devastated. It was the straw that broke the camel's back, and she told God that this was it— she was going to leave the faith. But as a last-ditch effort she decided to go to the artists' worship meeting (she was a graphic designer) and that if God didn't dramatically show up for her, then she was finished with him.

On the way to the meeting, she heard God say that *he* would be her husband now, and that things were going to be alright. But she disregarded it, believing it was all just in her head.

Then the rose petals landed on her. She told me that when she smelled them, they had the *exact same scent* as the rose petals that were scattered on her at her own wedding. She had picked that specific scent, and so had God.

Her faith was restored that day, because hidden in that scent that I had spent so much time getting right was a precious message from God just for her. A message so secret that only she would have been able to get it. This was the wedding proposal from Christ to her. He knew exactly how to touch this woman's heart in a way that was totally specific to her.

God had a way, a message, that had the power to cut right through all the hurt and show her that everything was going to be okay. He knew how to woo her back to himself. Someone could have prophesied a message over her, or she could have read a scripture, but that wouldn't have had the same impact. No, he wanted to send a clear message that was much more personal, a custom-made message just for her. And since she herself was a visual artist, what better way than a custom-made sculpture?

A number of people came up to me after that dramatic meeting, and showed me how each tiny aspect of the sculpture had been custom designed with various hidden messages that spoke to each of them in different ways. Every little detail had been layered with meaning that was specific and individual to the people who attended that day.

Obedience and creativity

I learned two profound lessons from that experience. First, that God has a prophetic language and can communicate in many different ways—even through the sense of smell. That container was a prophetic "word" for that woman, and others in that meeting, just the same as if someone stood up and pronounced "Thus saith the Lord" over them. From that day, I learned to never underestimate the creativity of God's love.

Second, as a recent speaker at our church put it, "God's blessings are tied up with our obedience. As we obey God, the blessings that he has stored up for us get released." There have been many other times in my life that I've had to obey God in something that didn't make a

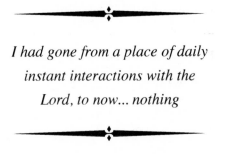

I had gone from a place of daily instant interactions with the Lord, to now... nothing

lot of sense to me, and each time the outcome has taken my breath away. Also, over the years, the Lord has given me blueprints to many different types of sculptures. Each of them has been an act of faith, never knowing ahead of time what the messages were or who they were for. They were simple acts of obedience.

Stepping out in faith is going to involve doing things you've never done before. It's going to put you in uncomfortable positions where you really don't know what's going to happen. It's going to require that you trust God in a new way.

I didn't know what would happen with this sculpture, and that's the wonderful thing. God is always full of surprises; he is always looking to bless people and to heal them. His love compels him to be like that. When you grab a hold of the flow of his love, you'll want to be like that too. It's a great way to live. You'll quickly discover the astounding creativity of God—he is so brimming full of new ideas you won't be able to keep up.

I encourage you to let go of any preconceived notions you have of how things will work out and just go with him. Let him do the work, and focus on what he's giving you to do. It will all work out in amazing ways that neither you nor I could ever dream of. It's one of the many blessings of being in relationship with Jesus.

PART TWO
Just to be with him

8.

Growing in the Wilderness

—————◆—————

*One thing I ask from the Lord, this only do I seek: that
I may dwell in the house of the Lord all the days of my
life, to gaze on the beauty of the Lord and to seek him in
his temple.*

Psalm 27:4

***

Sometimes it's in the desert seasons of life that we grow
the most; grow in a way that never could have happened
otherwise.

Desert seasons are when nothing appears to be happening
in your relationship with the Lord. You feel dry spiritually,
God does not appear to be talking to you, and your prayer
life becomes a chore rather than a delight. As a young man I
had experienced many miracles of healing, faith, and above

all of hearing God's voice—but one of the most profound lessons of my life came later, through three years of spiritual dryness, when God seemed completely absent. It was a total wilderness experience.

An unlikely couple

In my second year of art college, in January 1992, I decided to attend a Monday night "College and Careers" group at a large Pentecostal church in downtown Toronto. Around 150 young Christians would join together at this church every Monday night for worship, Bible study and fellowship, and it was really a happening place. Little did I know that this chance decision to attend would change the course of my life.

On that first Monday night, I was allocated to a group of newcomers who were attending the group for the first time. It included another newcomer called Amy. She was looking for a Christian community, having just moved back to Canada after completing her doctorate in Biology at Oxford University in England. We chatted a little and she learned that I was studying only a few blocks from her work at the university, where she was doing a post-doctoral fellowship. She suggested we meet for lunch.

Over the next few months this unlikely pair—the well-travelled scientist and the 21-year-old art student—met for lunch, went skating, hung out together, and fell in love. We were certainly a strange couple, and both sets of parents weren't quite sure what to make of us. But around 18 months later, in August 1993—after the many ups and downs of a typical budding relationship— Amy and I were married.

By the following year, we both had new career directions. I had graduated from art college and was embarking on a career as a sculptor, doing odd art-related jobs here and there, while Amy left academia and started a new career in the pharmaceutical business. We had a small basement apartment in downtown Toronto where we were very happy, but poor, since repaying student loans was a high priority. We lived in Toronto for the first six years of our married life, our time filled with church and social activities. The experience that most shaped our Christian journey was being involved in transforming our church into a cell-based church, where everyone met in small groups during the week. This training and experience would be invaluable to the two home-based churches (often referred to as "house church") that we would start many years later.

Professionally, my career as a sculptor was clearly not going to pay the bills, so a few years later I joined an inner-city mission organization where I led an arts program for homeless street youth. Although this gave me a regular job, like many missionaries I still needed to raise money for my salary, and that was extremely challenging. It was quite clear at this point that Amy's job was needed to keep us afloat, and that I needed to figure out what to do with my life.

Amy had always had the dream of living in Europe. She believed that if you have a vision, you need to put plans in place to achieve it—she is a businesswoman after all! So after years of strategic planning, we uprooted our comfortable life in Toronto and moved to the UK.

1999 was a year of radical change; we moved to the UK five weeks after the birth of our first daughter, Claire. Then, after six months in the UK (the length of Amy's maternity leave), Amy was offered a job at the head office of a large pharmaceutical company based in Basel, Switzerland. So within 12 months, we had become first-time parents, temporarily moved to the UK, returned to Toronto to sell and pack up our meagre worldly goods, then moved to Switzerland with a nine-month old baby, a cat and a shipping container of stuff. Many people, except Amy's mum, thought we were crazy; but we were following our dreams.

Spiritually dry

So, by early 2000 there I was—a stay-at-home, 29-year-old father, with no career or glossy coffee table book to my name, in a German-speaking country where everything worked differently, with a professional wife who was working and travelling almost constantly. I struggled to learn the language, and all the

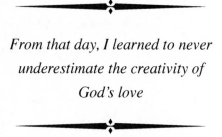

From that day, I learned to never underestimate the creativity of God's love

other local stay-at-home parents were Swiss mums. I had little in common with any of them. It was a very difficult time for me, and it certainly wasn't what I had imagined my life to be like.

We lived in a small village near Basel, Switzerland, and with very few English-speaking churches in our area, we settled into one around 20 kilometres north and over the border in Germany's Black Forest region. This large church was unusual, since around 95 percent of its Sunday morning population consisted of the staff and the students of the Christian boarding school associated with the church. Given our family background of Baptist (me), United Church (Amy) and Pentecostal (us as a married couple) we felt that we didn't really fit in anywhere. And this church did not encourage the use of spiritual gifts. We would drive there on a Sunday morning, listen to the message, and go home again without much sense of belonging. So, in a way, we were lost spiritually as well as being outsiders in this Christian community.

I had gone from a place of daily, instant interactions with the Lord as a teenager, to an adventurous, faith-filled Christian life during my twenties, to now ... nothing. It was a very long period of nothing, lasting from the ages of 29 to 32, and I felt that I had gone numb spiritually. At first I wasn't too worried, but over time I became deeply concerned. For a three-year period, I didn't feel that God highlighted any scripture, I didn't feel his presence in worship, my prayer time was uninteresting, and sermons were long and boring. This was a marked contrast to what had been going on before.

The thing that drove me crazy during this time was that I had no idea why the spiritual taps had been turned off. Had I sinned in some way? Had I offended the Lord over something? Was I carrying unforgiveness against someone? Had I missed something I was supposed to do? Had I been disobedient? Was it past failures (or "learning opportunities" as I call them) catching up to me? I had a long list of possible reasons, but I just didn't know which one it was. During this time, I focused on raising our daughter Claire, learning German and painting landscapes in oil.

In January 2003, Amy got a promotion so we relocated to Montreal, Canada, with our family. We now had two daughters; our second daughter, Alice, was born in Switzerland in January 2002. So there I was— at minus 20°C in the middle of winter, living in temporary accommodation under a sea of grey skies, in a house with two small children (Claire was four, Alice was one)—and a busy wife. If I'm honest, by this time I was angry with the Lord. What had been the point of those three years in Switzerland? It was supposed to have been a time of spiritual growth, of reaching out and touching others' lives. Instead it felt spiritually empty and meaningless, and now here we were, back where we started in Canada.

Out of the desert

Within a few months we had bought a new home in a town just off the west of the island of Montreal, and started attending a local Pentecostal church. We quickly became involved in the Christian community and attended as many English-speaking conferences as possible, since we felt spiritually starved of English-language services. One of these conferences marked the end of my three-year desert season. There, I finally came to the place where God wanted me, and during the ministry time, I got an answer from the Lord to the many questions I'd been asking.

The answer had nothing to do with the questions I had been asking myself; it turned out to be something else altogether. It was to do with my identity. My spiritual gifts—that is, the prophetic ability to hear and experience the Lord—had become the source of my Christian identity. In other words, the gift had become more important than the giver. Ouch!

Having spent three years in a place with no outlet for this gift, where my role was to be "nothing more" than a stay-at-home father, my sense of identity had been threatened. This perspective had crept up on me unintentionally, and I'd had no idea. During this conference, I had to come to a place where I was so thirsty for God's presence that I was willing to look at my heart from

I had spent three years thinking I was waiting for him, but actually he was waiting for me!

81

an uncomfortable direction, from a perspective that I was in denial about. I had to come to a place where I cried out to God that I didn't care if I ever prophesied over another person again, I just wanted more of him. The giver had to be more, much more, important than the gift.

The second I cried out to God, saying that all I wanted was him, I had a profound experience—the first in three years—where I was swept up into the waiting arms of Christ and sat on his lap like a little child. I had an encounter with him that was so real I could feel the texture of the fabric of his robes and, as his tears of joy flowed down his face and dripped onto mine, I could literally taste the saltiness in my mouth.

I had spent three years thinking I was waiting for him, but actually *he* was waiting for *me*! He had felt the pain of our disconnection even more deeply than I had.

That lesson, the product of three painful years in the wilderness, was simple: *he* is all we'll ever need. We must seek the giver not just his gifts. The purpose of spiritual gifts is not to make us feel better about ourselves because we think we're special. We're made in his image—that simple fact already makes us special! The purpose of spiritual gifts is to lead us into deeper relationship with him, and to serve him and his kingdom.

It's easier to find our sense of self-worth in what we *do* rather than who we *are*: children of God. This is the difference between *doing* and *being*. This is true for men and women. Men, especially, often find their identity in what they do, and for us it requires conscious decisions every day to choose to place our identity into our relationship with God. Certainly for me, doing things for God had become my spirituality. For women, their temptation is to find their identity within their relationships with others, especially family. For charismatic Christians (those who seek the *charismata* or gifts of the Holy Spirit) it's easy to focus on the gifts, our authority, our specific ministry, and so on. Yet that's not the goal. The goal is relationship with him. It's *all* about him.

That was the lesson I had to learn and it took three spiritually dry years to figure it out. It seemed like an endless three years. I love spiritual gifts, and I love seeing them used for the furtherance of God's kingdom; but I now understand their purpose better than I did before. When you see a person using the gift God has given them, whatever it is, you rejoice in your spirit and you hear heaven singing—but it's not because that person is so gifted. It's because God's character is being revealed. Now, above all titles, positions and power, I just value being in his presence.

The purpose of Christianity

The lesson I'd learnt in those three wilderness years became crystal clear to me several years afterwards, through another experience that had a deep impact on me and on the very structure of my faith. It wasn't the most flashy "fireworks" type of experience I've ever had but, as is often the case, it's more about what is said than how it's said. I

83

was carrying out a very spiritual exercise at the time: I was walking the dog.

As I walked our dachshund Coco through the streets near our home, I had my headphones on and was listening to worship music. About two minutes into the walk, I heard the Lord speak to me very softly—but clearly—and he asked me a question.

"What is the purpose of Christianity?"

This was such an unexpected question that it completely threw me off my walk, and I came to a dead stop mid-stride.

Pulling off my headphones, I replied, "Umm, ummm, I know this . . . It's the kingdom coming to earth. That's it, the kingdom . . . Oh wait, what about salvation? That's really important too, yeah, salvation, that's it! Hang on... what about healing? Can't forget about healing . . . Oh, and there's missionary work too. Wait, wait what about the Great Commission ...?"

This went on for a few minutes until a little light bulb came on inside my head. I realized: perhaps the Lord is asking me this question because he knows that I don't know the answer.

So I replied, "I don't know, Lord. Perhaps you could tell me."

I said that because I'd learnt something: when God asks you a question it's not because he's looking for the answer. He already knows the answer. Instead, he's looking for you to understand where your own heart is at. When you see the truth of where your heart is, you can see the invisible chains that bind you. Then he can set you free. His questions are just as revealing as his answers, if you let them speak to your heart. Since he *is* truth, everything he says contains a grain of who he is, and it's the truth that sets us free.

So he told me. He said one of the simplest and most profound things he's ever said to me. It had a deeper impact on how I live my Christian life than just about anything else:

"The purpose of Christianity is to just *be* with God."

As he said this, he showed me something in my mind's eye: I saw a young couple who want to get married. The reason they want marriage, rather than continuing to date each other, is that they want to *be* together.

He showed me that this desire to *be* together is the simplest and most basic expression of love. If you love someone you will naturally want to be with them. When I was dating Amy, sometimes we would just listen to each other breathing softly on the other end of the phone line. Being in each other's presence was enough. Being with Jesus is the same: it's enough to be with him, in the same room, even if he isn't saying anything: to simply know he's there.

I realized that I now needed a course correction. My purposes for Christianity had all involved doing things—good things, of course—but being busy doing all these things for God. Whereas God's purpose went much deeper and freed me from that burden of *doing*. The whole nature of our Christian faith can be summed up in just *being* together.

So simple and yet so profound.

During our life here on earth we get to practice just being together with God, and we'll continue to be together with him when we transition from this life into eternity.

So very simple and yet so beautiful.

Jesus described this eloquently in John 17, which is for me the most important chapter of the gospels:

> "My prayer is not for them alone. I pray also for those who will believe in me through their message, *that all of them may be one, Father, just as you are in me and I am in you.* May they also be in us so that the world may believe that you have sent me. I have given them the glory that you gave me, that they may be one as we are one — I in them and you in me — so that they may be brought to complete unity. Then the world will know that you sent me and have loved them even as you have loved me."

> John 17:20-23 (emphasis added)

Jesus prays that we may be "one", just as he is in the Father and the Father is in him. Jesus' mission to earth can be summed up like this: the restoration of oneness between all of God and all of mankind. In other words, God just wants us to *be* together.

I can't tell you how deep an effect this has had on me. It has put within my reach goals and standards of the Christian life that had felt at times impossible to achieve. It has also set a tone of mutual love and respect. For the young couple that the Lord showed me,

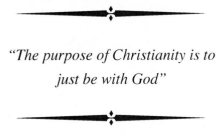

"The purpose of Christianity is to just be with God"

all they need to take the next step in their relationship, from dating to engagement to marriage, is the simplest product of love—the basic desire to *be* together.

This is the beating heart at the center of Christianity—the simple desire to be together with God.

It has formed the central pillar of my faith, and it's now what I speak about all the time. Christianity is not complicated; it's very simple. It's all about love and the expressions of real love. We don't need to stray too far from that. The beauty and simplicity of him loving you and you returning that love ... that relationship is so wonderful, and the key to everything else.

It's not about how big and successful your church is (or isn't), it's not about how many committees you are on, or what style of worship music you play, or how thoughtful your Bible studies are, although all of those are good. At the end of the day, it's about the simplicity of just being together with Jesus.

> Now this is eternal life: that they know you, the only true God, and Jesus Christ, whom you have sent.

John 17:3

9.

Seated with Him

◆

But because of his great love for us, God, who is rich in mercy, made us alive with Christ even when we were dead in transgressions—it is by grace you have been saved. And God raised us up with Christ and seated us with him in the heavenly realms in Christ Jesus...

Ephesians 2:4-6

***

If the whole purpose of Christianity is to *be* with God—this "oneness" that Jesus spoke about in John 17—what difference does that make when we pray?

Praying in the wrong direction

Although it's a few years ago now, I remember like yesterday a prayer meeting in my living room: it was the first time the Lord spoke to me about the direction of our prayers. After leaving the Pentecostal church we had attended for a few years (while living near Montreal), we were pastoring a house church that God had called us to start. In one of our meetings we were praying for a church member who was having marriage problems. We were calling out to God and being very vocal. In other words, we were all worked up and praying loudly and forcefully.

In the middle of my prayer, the Lord literally interrupted me by speaking clearly into my mind:

"You are praying in the wrong direction."

"What do you mean?" I asked, a bit offended by being interrupted.

"You're praying from earth towards heaven. You should be praying from heaven towards earth."

I immediately spoke this out loud to our group, and I remember their stunned silence. A sense of awe settled on the room and we all knew that we had heard from the Lord.

Although we had been corrected, no one felt reprimanded. Instead we wanted to sing, to shout and give each other high fives—it was as if a locked door that we'd been knocking on for years had suddenly flown open of its own accord. In this one moment, we'd been entrusted with a new understanding. I felt like I'd been struggling to

"You're praying from earth towards heaven. You should be praying from heaven towards earth"

read a map that wasn't making sense, only for someone to come along, take it out of my hands, and turn it around. In that moment God turned our map right side up.

He re-orientated our viewpoint and showed us that we had been limiting ourselves by our own self-imposed restrictions of separation from our God.

We were not to be lowly little believers stuck down on a sinful, dark earth, separated by an impassable chasm from the great and glorious kingdom of the risen God. No, we were suddenly *one* with him, and far from being stuck down below, we were reigning on high with him. We were the head and not the tail, above and not beneath. We were no longer the beggars weeping and wailing, desperate for the merest scrap from the master's table, or the tiniest drop of water to wet our parched lips.

Our eyes had been opened, and we looked around to discover we were seated with Christ.

> But because of his great love for us, God, who
> is rich in mercy, made us alive with Christ
> even when we were dead in transgressions—
> it is by grace you have been saved. And God
> raised us up with Christ and seated us with
> him in the heavenly realms in Christ Jesus...

> Ephesians 2:4–6

Being "seated with Christ in the heavenly realms" isn't just a theological statement: it's a key to relationship. In order to have a relationship you need to be in the same space together. This is what it means to *be* with God, to live in the oneness that Jesus spoke about. If he is in heaven and we are down on earth, then we are separated from him—but if we are *in* him, seated with him, and he is in us, then our perspective changes to his perspective. We begin to live out of that purpose of Christianity: just being with him. Our prayer and intercession begin to reflect that.

There is a place for earth-based prayers that reach up to heaven. Sometimes that's all we've got, and all we can do is to reach up. But we need to build an expectation in our hearts of that very important place of intercession: based out of heaven and directed towards the earth.

What God showed us that day wasn't a new prayer strategy—it's much bigger than that. He was showing us a key to his kingdom that he had already given us, but that we hadn't seen.

I believe Jesus prayed in this way, and I believe that we are to pray this way too. I believe that God wants us to pray from this heart position and mindset, because that is the fulfilment of his mission to restore relationship. Once that relationship is in process and starts to gain traction in our lives, it will bear fruit and result in real changes. We will no longer be living from the results of our sinful world but out of the reality of the new covenant.

Designed for relationship with God

Not only is it our *purpose* as human beings to be in relationship with God; relationship with him is built into our design. Every believer knows that they were created by God, but have you thought about the fact that you were designed by him too?

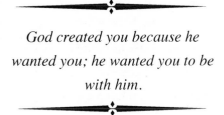

God created you because he wanted you; he wanted you to be with him.

What's the difference between "created" and "designed"? An artist creates. There may or may not be a purpose to that creation other than the pure pleasure of creating. But design is more goal-orientated. An artist may start with a blank canvas and let the art develop organically; a designer is working to fulfil a set of criteria. Every designer is trying to fulfil a need. There is something that needs to be fixed, and they are coming up with their design to fix that problem. It might be a visual style, or a functional problem; but there is always purpose to design.

God the designer had his endpoint in mind before he even started the creation of the world. God desired relationship. That was the goal, the design criteria if you will, before he even started. You were designed to be able to meet that goal of a relationship, a full relationship with God.

Every good design must not only be beautiful but it must also meet its functional requirements. So if I designed a chair, for example, but my design wasn't strong enough to sit on, then it's not a good design. God, on the other hand, declared that his design—us—is good. He says we are not only beautiful and pleasing, but functional too—and our function is to be in relationship with him.

You were built from the very beginning with the ability to be in relationship with God. That is the main reason you have a spirit. Scripture says that God is spirit (John 4:24)—so if you didn't also have a spirit it would be impossible for you to make a connection with God. The reason you do have a spirit is so that the opportunity for fully developed relationship exists; and then the choice is yours whether to pursue it or not.

The message of evolutionary theory is that you were just a random development; you could have turned out this way or you could have turned out another. Being created by God, however, contains a very different message: it says you were wanted, cherished and loved before you began, and that you were created on purpose. These two messages—one of the randomness of evolution, and the other of the intentionality of God—are opposite to each other. Don't fall into the trap of blending the two.

God created you because he wanted you; he wanted you to be with him.

Connecting with God, spirit to Spirit

Having a spirit is what makes relationship with God possible. It's also what makes us alive. Our spirit is made in the image of God; it's his breath that he imparted into us.

94

Do you know you have a spirit that is distinct from your soul and body? If your spirit and soul were the same thing, then they wouldn't be listed as separate items in the New Testament:

> May God himself, the God of peace, sanctify you through and through. May your whole *spirit, soul, and body* be kept blameless at the coming of our Lord Jesus Christ.
>
> 1 Thessalonians 5:23 (emphasis added)

Many people confuse soul and spirit. They use the words interchangeably to mean the same thing, but in fact they are quite different.

Your spirit is defined as the God-given, spiritual aspect of yourself that makes relationship with God possible. Being made in the image of God, your spirit is the reflection of the Holy Spirit. Your soul, however, is your mind, will, and emotions.

As you are made in the image of God who is a spirit, it would be more accurate to say that you *are* a spirit, who *has* a soul, and is *in* a body.[1] And your spirit was given as a reflection of the divine nature of God for the purpose of

---

[1] I've heard this taught by Patricia King, author of *Spiritual Revolution* (Destiny Image Publishers, 2006).

developing a relationship with him—through Jesus. We must always keep our eye on the prize; Jesus himself is the prize.

> Jesus answered, "I am the way and the truth and the life. No one comes to the Father except through me."

John 14:6

Jesus said he is the narrow gate and the narrow way, and that nobody gets to the Father except through him. Jesus is the doorway, and on the other side is the Father. Where is the Father? In heaven. Where is Jesus now? He ascended into heaven (Acts 1:9). So if you want to get to the Father then you have to go through Jesus in heaven. And you can do that through your spirit, because your spirit is seated with Christ in the heavenly realms (Eph 2:6).

This is a function of your spirit. The moment you got saved, your spirit went from being dead to being alive. It went from being blind to being able to see. It went from darkness to light. And what happened was that your spirit, in a sense, climbed up onto Jesus' lap while he was sitting on his throne— the "mercy seat"—and now you are "seated with him in the heavenly realms".

The purpose of Christianity is to be with God. He takes that very literally.

God jealously longs for the spirit that he breathed into you to be with him, and to be with him right now. You were created to meet that design criteria: "But whoever is united with the Lord is one with him in spirit" (1 Cor 6:17).

The amplified version says, "But the person who is united to the Lord becomes one spirit with him."

I'm still trying to get my head around this verse. But this I do know: to be with somebody is the most basic, simple, purest expression of love.

And God really, really wants to be with you.

You are more spiritual than you think

People often say to me: "I'm having trouble hearing from God. God never says anything to me. I can't connect with God. He feels so distant. Everybody else has these wonderful experiences with him, but never me. How do I know if God is talking to me?"

Perhaps you feel the same way. Perhaps you don't feel like a spiritual person. You might tell me that you have never had a spiritual experience in your life.

Well, this idea might be completely foreign to you: but you are more spiritual than you think.

On most days I don't feel like I'm a spirit with a soul living in a body. I'm caught up in the very practical, mundane

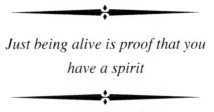

Just being alive is proof that you have a spirit

things of life: cooking, cleaning and running the kids to and from school and their various activities. The vast majority of my time every day is firmly planted in the practical day-to-day issues of living in this world. Nonetheless, I have been designed for relationship with God, and so have you.

How do I know that you are a spiritual person who has a spirit? Let's start with this—without your spirit you'd be dead:

> As the body without the spirit is dead, so faith
> without deeds is dead.

> James 2:26

> And when Jesus had cried out again in a loud
> voice, he gave up his spirit.

> Matt 27:50

So just being alive is proof that you have a spirit. And it is in your spirit that the image of God is most accurately reflected, as a direct gift and impartation of who he is as spirit. This was God's design so you can be with him now, and continue to be with him after your body passes away, or he comes again when you receive a new body. And if you have faith in Jesus, your spirit is truly alive and seated with Christ.

Some Christians have spent their whole lives crying out to God, "Why don't you speak to me?" They don't realize that they are praying the wrong prayer. This is praying in the wrong direction. It is not true that God doesn't speak to you, that you can't make a connection with God, that you can't feel his presence. Since the moment you got saved your spirit has not left his presence; he has never stopped talking to you. As we saw in the section above, our spirit—which is part of you—is spending its days sitting right beside Jesus himself (Eph 2:6) contemplating his glory:

> Now the Lord is the Spirit, and where the Spirit of the Lord is, there is freedom. And we all, who with unveiled faces *contemplate the Lord's glory*, are being transformed into his image with ever-increasing glory, which comes from the Lord, who is the Spirit.
>
> 2 Corinthians 3:17-18 (emphasis added)

The problem isn't that God isn't speaking to you. The problem is a disconnect inside of us—this breakdown and separation between soul and spirit. Since scripture tells us that God is Spirit, if we are completely out of touch with our own God-given spirit, that isn't going to help us get to know him. Your soul, body and spirit must work together for you to be able to be a whole person and build relationship with God effectively.

For some people this is easy and natural. For others this is really and truly difficult. Just as we can easily be out of touch with our feelings or emotions, we can easily be out of touch with our spirit. That doesn't mean our spirit isn't there; it just means that the connections between soul and spirit are underdeveloped. In the same way that our muscles need to be exercised, our feelings need to be expressed, and our connections to our spirit need to be developed. If you only use your mind (which is part of your soul) you will be operating with one hand tied behind your back.

We have to get in touch with this important part of ourselves; we have to develop our connection between spirit and soul. Getting in touch with our spiritual side is not permission to get weird or "New Age". It is permission to get to know God. That is why we *have* a spirit.

At the end of this book you'll find a practical section suggesting ways to hear God's voice. Taking the steps outlined in those chapters is one way of getting in touch with our own spiritual side, and building that soul-spirit connection.

10.

Supernatural Hunger

---◆---

You, God, are my God, earnestly I seek you;
I thirst for you, my whole being longs for you,
in a dry and parched land where there is no water.

Psalm 63:1

***

After my wilderness period then breakthrough with the Lord, I entered into a season of supernatural, exponential growth. Through his grace, God gave me an insuppressible, insatiable hunger for more of him and his presence. I'm now grateful for those three spiritually dry years. They helped to fuel my hunger for him, and led to the lesson of "seeking him above the gifts" that changed my life—so, paradoxically, as I began to seek God for his presence rather than his gifts, he poured out his gifts on me more than ever.

A man on a mission

A relative of mine, Vicky, had started attending a church in Hamilton, Ontario, called Eagle Worldwide. They are a training center for spiritual gifts, and it was here that I received intensive training in the prophetic, working with the Holy Spirit and was later ordained. The training seemed to be custom made just for me, and I quickly discovered that I didn't know nearly as much as I'd thought. I

I needed to stretch my faith every day

bought all the teaching CDs, took them home and listened to them over and over until I could quote them by heart. For a whole year, almost every day, while I painted in my art studio I didn't listen to music—I would play the teaching CDs on repeat until they were worked into my spirit and not just my head.

I was pressing in harder into him than I had ever in my life. I wanted —no, *needed*—to stretch my faith every day. It was like some personal contest to see how far I could get spiritually. It didn't take long for the results to come.

Suddenly, I found myself having the opportunity to regularly prophesy over people. More regular visions and prophetic signs or experiences began to happen. I went to every conference that I was able to go to, and I was going from glory to glory. I was a man on a mission!

Soon I was getting "words of knowledge" about people's illnesses. I remember lying in bed at night, trying to go to sleep, and the Lord would ask me, "What would you do if you were at church and I told you that there was someone there who had pain in their leg?"

I would say, "I don't know."

And I would see myself walking up to the front of the church and calling this out. I would see people coming up for prayer and receiving healing. It's really hard to get to sleep when you are having this kind of dialogue every night for weeks on end!

Then a guest speaker come to our church; it was the well-known Canadian evangelist, Bill Prankard. He had a large ministry, and people he prayed for were often healed. I had volunteered to help with ministry at this meeting, so while he preached I was waiting at one side for the ministry time. While I waited I kept receiving lists from the Lord: "There's someone here with heart problems, someone with elbow pain, headaches" and so on.

Two minutes later, Bill stood up and started calling out the exact same list as I'd just heard, and even in the same order! This was really astounding to me. He was praying over all these people and many healings were taking place. This was a real confirmation to me that God was doing something, and I needed to take it seriously.

It wasn't long before I was up at the front at meetings myself, calling out lists of illnesses and pains, and the people who came forward to receive prayer were getting healed. I could feel God's power moving through me, but also through the room. God would show me who he was going to touch and often what direction they were going to fall. This was really useful so helpers could be directed to catch people before they hit the ground. I would attend Bible studies and visit other churches, and the Holy Spirit would do his work in these places too. I can tell you that it was really exciting to see God moving!

God is always looking to break out into his church and his people in new ways. He wants to show himself to be alive—the risen Christ! And he wants to use you to do it, to demonstrate it by living it out.

It only takes a spark to start a fire: be that spark! Don't just look to someone else to give you the kind of faith you're looking for: live it yourself. It doesn't matter what your gifts are—there is no upper limit to faith. There's no part of Christianity that says "you've reached the maximum and there

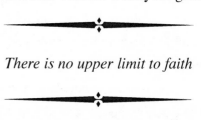

There is no upper limit to faith

isn't any more". No, Christ is limitless. Go and be a miracle worker, be someone who raises the dead and preaches to the poor; but most of all be someone who truly loves God and wants to be with him. And don't wait—start today.

An open heaven

In our house church we were so blessed to be with a group of people who were hungry, deeply hungry, for the Lord. The presence of God at these meetings was wonderful. We didn't have a worship team so we just put on a CD; yet those times of worship were powerful. I remember for three whole months I was in deep repentance during worship. All I could do was to lie on the floor or curl up in a little ball on the carpet weeping over the greater church who had drifted away from her first love, Jesus. Even now, over ten years later, I still feel it very deeply.

We had an "open heaven", and—especially after my wilderness experience—I was determined to make the most of it. Everyone would be given spiritual homework to do during the week. Usually it was a simple question to ask God, and if you got something, to bring it back and share. (This "homework" and how to do it yourself is described in more detail in the last section of this book.)

It was incredible what people got! They were having angelic visitations in their bedrooms; dramatic encounters with God; strangers walking up to them and prophesying the answers to them; and what they received was heart-wrenchingly beautiful. We would cry our way through meeting after meeting. Not only that, but one person would have been dealing with an issue, and another would separately get a dream that was the answer to what the first person was dealing with. This probably happened three or four times per meeting and we met twice a week. This went on for a few years, and this time completely redefined what "normal Christianity" was. The presence of God was tangible in our midst. His hand was at work in our lives on a daily basis. It was truly an incredible time and a time of tremendous spiritual growth.

For me personally, my prayer times took on a whole new level of significance. They became all about just being with God. His presence was so powerful, even in my own living room. Often I couldn't get past saying, "Dear God..." and his presence would fill the room. Sometimes he would be there before I could even start praying. This wasn't about prayer time anymore; it was about stepping into the presence of the Lord.

What the Lord showed me in those encounters is what I would eventually teach others about; I'd read an account of what had happened from my journal and then teach what God asked me to share. These encounters with the risen Christ had such a deep impact on me that I'm still unpacking them, even all these years later. Every day I meditate on them, and I'm still growing, still learning about how wonderful our Lord Jesus is.

11.

Wait in my Presence

That same night the Lord said to him, "Take the second
bull from your father's herd, the one seven years old. Tear
down your father's altar to Baal and cut down the Asherah
pole beside it. Then build a proper kind of altar to the Lord
your God on the top of this height. Using the wood of the
Asherah pole that you cut down, offer the second bull as a
burnt offering."

Judges 6:25-26

***

As I continued in this season of exponential spiritual
growth, leading our house church near Montreal and
speaking at small conferences, the Lord started teaching me
about obedience.

His plan, his way

When I'm asked to speak at a conference, my goal is that people would have their own encounters with God; so it makes no sense for me to sit down and come up with my own plan. That's absolutely the last thing I want to do. I want to hear from the Lord and do his plan, his way. I want to be on a mission from God!

One day I got a phone call from my friends Jacques and Jo-Anne, asking me to come and speak at their retreat center for a weekend conference (I had already spoken at conferences there several times before). The conference was in about three months' time, and I would need to preach about six times over one weekend; it was an intense schedule. As usual, I took it to the Lord to see if he wanted me to go. He told me clearly to go, but when I asked him how I should prepare, and what he wanted me to speak about, the answer was simply "Wait in my presence."

Ok, wait in his presence. That's fine—I can do that.

So I waited in his presence for a few weeks. Then I asked again—same answer.

"Just wait in my presence."

When preparing for something like this you might think that it's just a case of listening to the Lord and copying down what he says and in thirty minutes you're done. Sometimes it is that simple, but most of the time it takes me many weeks of prayer, seeking the Lord, and lots of studying scripture. So typically, to prepare six messages for a weekend conference usually takes me a full three months of daily, intense, intentional seeking of both the presence and word of the Lord.

I never want to just bring some sort of intellectual message based on choosing a scripture and picking three points from it—where's the fun in that? I want to grow in the Lord too. I don't want to just speak a message, I want to live it. It's about going on a spiritual journey with the Lord, engaging in dialogue with him, and the story that comes out of that journey—that journey is the message. That process, the development and personal spiritual growth that came out of this dialogue was what these conferences were all about, and how I continue to prepare my talks to this day.

At one month before the conference I had nothing from the Lord. I'd been waiting in his presence (perhaps a bit impatiently) for two months. He'd talked to me about lots of other things, but none of them were related to the conference. Jacques and Jo-Anne called me and asked what title they should give the conference for their advertising, and I just didn't know. I took it back to the Lord, and got the same answer. "Wait in my presence."

Now it's two weeks before the conference and I'm sweating.

Then it's one week—still the same answer.

Now I'm feeling very stressed. Jacques and Jo-Anne are calling and wanting to know what I'm speaking about and I've got zip! I'm really nervous and so are they.

Finally, three days before the conference, the Lord tells me to look up Gideon.

I'm like, "Oh thank God, finally something!"

So I look up Gideon, and this part stands out to me:

> That same night the Lord said to him, "Take the second bull from your father's herd, the one seven years old. Tear down your father's altar to Baal and cut down the Asherah pole beside it. Then build a proper kind of altar to the Lord your God on the top of this height. Using the wood of the Asherah pole that you cut down, offer the second bull as a burnt offering."
>
> Judges 6:25-26

He tells me, "See how Gideon had to chop down and burn the family idols before he could be used by me?"

"Yes, okay, I see that."

"Well, I want to use these people at the conference to bring my kingdom—but before I can use them, they need to get rid of their idols too."

"Okay," I say, feeling a bit strange about this, "by the way, Lord, what idols? Do people still have idols?"

I was not convinced that God's plan was a good idea. In fact, I thought it was a very bad idea indeed

He responds, "You'll know how big an idol is by how much fuss you make when I take it away."

He goes on, "In the basement of the retreat center there is a stack of firewood. Have everyone pick a piece of firewood, write the names of their idols on the firewood, and we're going to have a campfire."

"We're going to what?!"

So he explained to me what to speak about for the entire weekend conference, and laid it all out, just like that.

Now we had done some crazy things at conferences in the past, but this plan took the cake as the most unusual by far. I was not convinced that this was a good idea. In fact, I thought it was a very bad idea indeed. However, it's not about what I think—my job is to listen and obey.

Bonfire

When we got to the retreat center, which was out in the country, we pulled up in the driveway and there was this huge pile of tree branches, brush and barn boards all piled up like a tepee outside in their front yard, ready to be burnt. It was about six feet tall. As I spoke with Jacques, the organizer, he apologized to me about all the wood.

"I was going to burn all this before everyone got here, as I've been cleaning up the place for the conference. But when I went to light it up, the Lord told me to wait."

"Oh," I said. "I know why." I started explaining about the plan "…well, you see, we have to have this campfire and burn some idols…"

He seemed about as skeptical as I felt, but he said, "Okay, let's do it."

I was nervous about this, but my commitment to the Lord was that we were doing his plan, his way. I'm not interested in coming up with my own message; I'm on a mission from God and here to do his will, not my own.

I preached my heart out, and the presence of the Lord was so strong, people were falling out of their chairs. I preached about how God wants to use us to build his kingdom. That, like Gideon, he has chosen us and called us "mighty" even before we have done anything to deserve that, because he can see the end of the story even while we are still at the beginning.

I asked the people, "Do you want to be used by God?" and everyone was cheering and clapping and shouting. I asked them, "Do you want to be used by God the way Gideon was used?" and they kept on cheering.

I said, "Well if you do, then you have to give up your idols, just like Gideon had to. We can recognize an idol in our lives by how attached we are to it—valuing it above God himself. It's easy to identify an idol. Just ask yourself, how much fuss would you make if God took it away?"

People got a bit quieter at that point.

So I asked Jacques to stand up, as his ministry was all about inner healing and dealing with "strongholds" in people's lives. He knew better than anyone that it's possible for something to be an idol in our lives, even if there isn't any little statue associated with it. He had no trouble giving a thorough explanation of how we can make anything into an idol; anything that we place above God. He told us how he and Jo-Anne deal with this in almost every person who comes to them for ministry.

Afterwards, everyone got their piece of firewood, wrote the name of their idol on it—things like money, jobs, cars, reputation, fear of what others think of us and so on— and we went outside and started to pile them up on the existing stack of tree branches and barn wood. By then it was pretty late at night.

Jacques and I actually discussed whether we should light it up with a match, or call down fire from heaven. The presence of the Lord was that strong that it

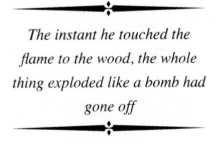

The instant he touched the flame to the wood, the whole thing exploded like a bomb had gone off

felt like fire from heaven was a real possibility. Anyway, we decided to light the bonfire with a match. Jacques crumpled a piece of newspaper into a long taper and lit the end of it.

The instant he touched it to the wood, the whole thing exploded like a bomb had gone off. It didn't light up—it *detonated!*

When you stand very close to a huge explosion you actually feel the force of it hitting your chest as much as you hear it with your ears. And it was loud. Everyone would have heard it for miles around. The whole retreat center building was shaken. In that moment, while time seemed to slow down, I remember seeing the glass of the retreat center windows bounce in their frames—it was amazing that none of them were broken. Everyone who was still in the house came spilling out onto the lawn, and we all stood in awe at this sign from God.

Later we discovered boxes of books had literally been knocked off shelves on the far side of the house, the force of the blast was so strong.

One of the miraculous things about this is that Jacques, who lit the fire and was standing right beside it, was totally unhurt. Unlike a normal explosion, none of the firewood, branches or flames were flung outwards. Instead the explosion went straight upwards, forming a spiralling column of flame as tall as the two-story retreat center!

I remember a cardboard banana box that was on the ground beside the bonfire getting sucked into the updraft of the flames, catching fire as it went up into the air. I was wondering where it was going to land, but it never came down—just disappeared into the night sky.

You could never have predicted this; God had his own plan for this event. Had I gone with my own ideas, then this would not have happened. God clearly wanted to shake the heavens and the earth, and he wanted to do it his way. This was an explosion in both the physical and supernatural realms.

It was an unmistakable supernatural sign from God that he was breaking the power of these idols and establishing his throne here on the earth. And I learned that God's way is always better than my ways.

12.

Continuing the Journey

They gave Moses this account: "We went into the land to which you sent us, and it does flow with milk and honey! Here is its fruit. But the people who live there are powerful, and the cities are fortified and very large."

Numbers 13:27-28

***

The event I described in the previous chapter would not have happened if I hadn't listened and obeyed, even though I was quite uncomfortable with the whole thing. I couldn't listen to the voice of fear; I had to choose faith and obedience to the Lord above my feelings and worries.

Travelling to points unknown

In obedience it's almost guaranteed that you won't know ahead of time how it's going to work out. God doesn't often give you all the steps that you'll need to take laid out in front of you—you usually only get the first step. It's always a step into the unknown, a step into a path whose destination is unclear. We just have the promise of God that all things work out for those who love him (Rom 8:28).

This is the place where faith and obedience join hand in hand. "Faith" is an action word that requires you to take a step into the unknown. If there's no action, then it isn't really faith.

It's like the saying, "If you want to walk on water, you have to get out of the boat."

Rarely does God call us to journey to a land that we know and are familiar with; he calls us to unknown places. These places are usually filled with giants. Like the Israelites, we have to overcome our fear and constantly learn to trust in God in new ways.

The disciples were each called with a "Come, follow me" invitation. There were no detailed descriptions of the benefits and responsibilities; no five-year plan describing the journey that they would go on. They were just called out of one life and into another.

This is usually how it works with God. We are called to die to the old self and its ways and to be resurrected into a new life. We get called to the person of Christ. The step of obedience of "Come, follow me" gets reapplied over and over in new ways—deeper ways. Each layer requires us to die to the ways of sin and death and get released into new life in new ways that we didn't understand before.

Very truly I tell you, unless a kernel of wheat falls to the ground and dies, it remains only a single seed. But if it dies, it produces many seeds. Anyone who loves their life will lose it, while anyone who hates their life in this world will keep it for eternal life. Whoever serves me must follow me; and where I am, my servant also will be. My Father will honor the one who serves me.

John 12:24-26

Imagine the blessings that the Israelites would have missed if they had chosen to stay in Egypt. Or if they had given up when being chased down by Pharaoh and his armies. Or if they had turned back and not crossed the Jordan. Or if they had not taken the land.

When you say "Yes" to God in salvation, this is not the end of the journey—it is the beginning. It's through faith that we embark on this journey; faith is what will take you from one place to the next. If you don't have faith, then you remain stuck in the same place, because faith has movement built into it.

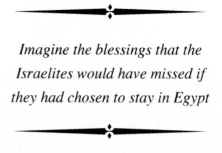

Imagine the blessings that the Israelites would have missed if they had chosen to stay in Egypt

Obedience will always call you to leave the old behind. To take a journey of faith, even though at times it will be unclear, you will be leaving a form of slavery and getting released into a new freedom and inheritance.

It is only through the journey of faith, the going through of the process, that we prove to ourselves the greatness and the faithfulness of God. It is through that process that the greatness of who God is is revealed to us. It is through this journey that our own story changes from "I *believe* that God is..." to "I *know* God is..." because he has proven it to me.

God has a plan for your life. It's an amazing plan which is so big that only he is able to accomplish it: a God-sized plan for your life. When you get a glimpse of how big that plan is you'll probably run away, just like Jonah, because it's obvious you can't make it happen. Only he can make it happen. But if you can look beyond the plan you'll see something else, something even more profound—Christ himself. God's plan is just the vehicle, the process by which you are to get to know him, get to trust him in a deeper way than you ever would on your own. His incredible, God-sized plan for your life, and the journey of faith that will be required to fulfil it, is the process that he uses to build relationship. That's why he says that *he*'s the way, the gate, the narrow path, and so on.

Tell your own story

My own journey with the Lord is far from over, and there are too many stories of the wonderful faithfulness of God to fit into this short book. Amy and I are once again living in Switzerland with our two teenage daughters, Claire and Alice; and for me, putting my story to paper is part of a new direction the Lord is taking me in.

There are no short-cuts to proving for yourself that Jesus is everything he says he is (and also so much more). My story, and that of others, can be stepping stones along your path — but the fulfilment of your own mission will ultimately be the revealing and unveiling of the truth of the nature of God in your *own* life. That's relationship.

I encourage you to share your own story. There is power in sharing the story of your journey with others, because it's your process of knowing God. "If God can do it for you, then maybe he can do it for me, too." It's sharing our stories — our own journeying with God — that forms a catalyst in other peoples' hearts. It can be what causes them to weigh anchor and cast off from their own shore of unbelief, and take their own journey with God, proving to themselves that not only is God faithful but that he's everything he says he is and more.

As I've shared my story on these pages, I hope that it's acted as a catalyst for you. If it has, pass it on — share your own journey with others. The story of your journey with God has the power to plant a seed into the hearts of those who hear it. Stories like yours contain a mustard seed of faith. That tiniest of seeds, a seed almost too small to see, has a special quality: it has the power to move mountains.

PART THREE
Your Turn to Hear his voice

13.
Learning to Hear his Voice

———————◆———————

Call to me and I will answer you and tell you great and
unsearchable things you do not know.

Jeremiah 33:3

***

H aving a deep, daily relationship with God and hearing
his voice is not just for a few special people—it's for
everyone. Learning to hear his voice is a key step to developing a life-sustaining relationship with him. After all, you
can't have a relationship with someone if you're not willing
to listen to what they have to say!

God speaks through scripture and through the Holy Spirit,
who he sent to us as our counselor when Jesus left this earth.
The Holy Spirit lives inside each believer, and one of his roles
is to "…teach you all things and…remind you of everything

I have said to you" (John 14:26). Therefore, the Holy Spirit is your connector to God.

I've written this practical section to help every believer learn to listen to God for themselves. It's pretty straightforward. The basic idea is to take time to be with God, ask him a question, wait for the answer, and write down

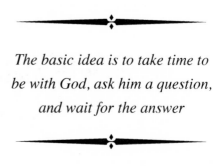

The basic idea is to take time to be with God, ask him a question, and wait for the answer

the first thing that comes into your mind. It's simple, but it works.

This is not a spiritual exam where there is only one right answer. In any relationship, asking an open-ended question (that is, a question that does not have a "yes" or "no" answer) leads to a dialogue, and it's through these dialogues that a deep, meaningful relationship is born. Questions are merely a means to an end, with the end being a deeper relationship with God that encompasses all of you. That's why being actively engaged in a dialogue with God is so important.

During our early house church days in Canada, when we first started asking God questions and entering into real dialogues with him, the results were profound. We gave everyone in the group a relationship-oriented question each week to ask God—for example, "'Why do you love me?" or "Tell me something about yourself" or "What would you like to talk about today?"—and to wait on him for an answer. And the answers came. Sometimes they came right away; sometimes they didn't. Sometimes the answers came in words, sometimes in images, sometimes through poetry. But I remember that we often cried our way through the whole meeting because the answers people received were so deep, and had such an impact, that we would never be the same again.

Five steps to listening

At its heart, Christianity isn't a club, or a set of moral values, or an activity you attend once a week — it's a relationship between you and God. Since communication is key to relationship, and the most important part of communication is the ability to listen, this whole exercise is about loving God by learning to listen to him.

To really listen to someone is a sign of respect. It means to stop always trying to get your point across first, slow down, close your mouth and open your ears. It isn't an easy thing to do. For the vast majority of people, prayer has turned into a basic needs request form. But if you were in God's shoes what would you prefer? Someone who is simply putting in their daily request for this and that, or someone who is seeking to actually get to know you?

Step 1. Set up a listening place

Find yourself a quiet place, for half an hour or so if you can — anywhere that separates you from the busyness of daily life. It could be a comfortable chair, the floor with a mat and pillow, or even a hot bath; or if home is busy, a walk or a park bench. Useful things to have with you are a Bible, some way of taking notes, and worship music. If you use a mobile device for any of the above, take care not to get side-tracked. Putting your mobile on "airplane" mode can at least stop incoming messages.

Step 2. Deal with distractions

A key to hearing God is, "Be still, and know that I am God" (Ps 46:10a).

Even away from our mobile devices, TVs and other electronic gadgets, getting into a place where we can "be still" is a big challenge. Planning, worrying, and nagging regrets send our minds hurrying all over the place. But part of being still before the Lord is being in the here and now, being fully present to him, with everything that makes

> *It's like going out to dinner with someone you love and refusing to check your phone every five minutes*

you who you are. It's like going out to dinner with someone you love and refusing to check your phone every five minutes. By focusing on the Lord, and putting all your distractions aside, you are fully available. You are sending a message to God: "Lord, you are more important to me than all this other stuff that's going on."

One way to deal with internal distractions is to acknowledge what they are and write them down. This approach gives our minds permission to set them aside for a time. If your mind is "fidgeting", try asking yourself the following questions. When you ask them, the best approach is to write down the first things that come to your mind. Do not over-think this exercise.

Am I worried or fearful? Write down what you're worried about. Is it family members, job, school or finances? Make a list of whatever comes to mind.

Am I planning? Write down any pressing activities that may be distracting you—this is typically our "to do" list, and all these things usually pull us away from focusing on God.

Am I angry or hurting? Has someone or something made you angry or hurt you? Do you keep replaying a certain situation over and over again in your mind? Write down the names of those you are angry with and/or have hurt you.

The act of writing these down might be enough to free your mind from distractions. If not, here are some ways to address them:

I'm worried. Take each item and give it to the Lord, asking for greater faith for this area. Literally hand each worry to God. If you like, you could write each worry down on a separate piece of paper and put it in a jar labelled, "For God to take care of."

I'm fearful. Take each fear and give it to God, and again ask for greater faith is this area. Be truthful to yourself and God; after all, he knows all about your fears already.

I'm planning. Now that you have written out your "to do" list you can set it aside and focus on the Lord. You can go back to it later.

I'm angry and/or hurt. Unforgiveness is a major blockage to deepening your relationship with God and to hearing from him. Later in this chapter you'll find a section on how to overcome common blockages to hearing God's voice, including how to fully forgive and be free to move forward with him.

Step 3. Dialogue through worship

Worship isn't fundamentally about music; it's about positioning ourselves before God and coming into his presence. As we worship in song, we lift God up in our hearts, and stop thinking about ourselves and our lives in order to focus on him. This positions the Lord in his rightful place in our hearts, and it positions ourselves in relation to him. This naturally puts us in a place to be filled with his presence and to hear him speak.

To dialogue through worship, you'll need some means of playing music — perhaps your phone, CD or MP3 player — and the lyrics to a worship song that you love. You could start by playing the song once or twice, singing along if you wish. Next, while it plays softly on repeat in the background, go through the lines one by one — not singing them but praying them, making the words your own, and lifting each line up to the Lord as your prayer.

Alternatively, you could worship with a favourite psalm. A good way to do this is read through the whole psalm once relatively quickly; then again slowly, one stanza at a time, as you give the words to God in worship. Pause after each stanza to listen to what God has to say, or to let the words sink in. Then read it a third time, slowly, giving a different emphasis to each sentence. Let its meaning flow into you. Give that meaning back up to God.

Whether using a song or a psalm, pause after each line to listen with your heart. Don't worry if you don't think God is speaking to you at this point. However, if you do hear that still, small voice inside or see an image in your spirit—perhaps an unexpected word, phrase, or mental image—write it down immediately. Don't worry about evaluating it yet. Just try to capture that moment. Then take the next line and lift it up, making it your prayer, and again take a moment to receive back. It's like waves on a beach— the wave rolls in, then it washes back out. It's the same during a dialogue. One person speaks and the other listens, then it's reversed.

After you're finished, take a moment to review what you wrote down. Ask the Lord if there's anything else he would like to add. If at this point you don't think that what you've written is from the Lord, that's okay. Just put it aside and don't beat yourself up. (There is more below about working out whether or not you are hearing God's voice.) Then finish by responding in worship.

Step 4. Build your faith that God will speak

Before taking this further, it's worth making the first three steps a regular practice: finding a quiet place away from everyday life, dealing with distractions, and dialoguing through worship. When you are used to them and finding it easier to still yourself before God, you're ready for the next step.

First bring yourself into God's presence as described in steps 1 to 3 above. Second, simply write down your immediate response to this question. Don't think about it—just write down the first thing that comes into your mind:

Is God *really* interested in speaking to me?

Let go of what you think you are supposed to answer and try to find out what you honestly believe. Often this is the first thing that pops into your head. Look at your honest, written answer, then read the following scriptures:

> "My sheep listen to my voice; I know them,
> and they follow me. I give them eternal life,
> and they shall never perish; no one will snatch
> them out of my hand."
>
> John 10:27-28

"Call to me and I will answer you and tell
you great and unsearchable things you do
not know."

Jeremiah 33:3

How does your written answer to the question above
compare to these Bible verses? Do you believe that God is
interested in speaking to you? If the answer is no, and you
feel that God is distant and uninterested, use these scriptures
to help you. Read these scriptures again then paraphrase them
by putting yourself into them. Read them out loud three times,
each time going slower. Let them sink into your heart and
make them your own. Here is what this might look like:

"I am one of the Lord's sheep and I am one
who hears his voice. He knows me and I
follow him. He gives me eternal life and so I
will never die. No one can ever snatch me out
of the Lord's hand."

"When I call to the Lord he answers me
and tells me great and hidden things that I
didn't know."

It's important to develop listening with faith. We may
need to remind ourselves of this every time we ask God to
speak to us, so that we fully expect an answer. Listen with the

intent of hearing, believing that God is not only fully capable of speaking to you, but that he actually wants to speak with you, and that you are capable of hearing.

Step 5. Ask questions

Now you're ready to ask the Lord some questions.

Perhaps the most fundamental question anyone can ask God is, "Lord, who are you?"—as I accidentally discovered. This is a great question to ask. It's also a huge question, and the answer is as big as God himself. So we

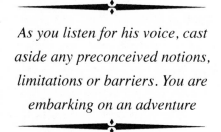

As you listen for his voice, cast aside any preconceived notions, limitations or barriers. You are embarking on an adventure

can break it down into smaller questions, like the ones I've suggested below.

This time, like the worship dialogue, take a moment between each line to let him respond. Write down what you get, even if you're not sure whether it's God speaking or your own imagination. Remember to write the first thing that comes to mind—do not over-think!

Thank you Lord that I can hear your voice. Lord, how can I hear your voice better?

Thank you Lord that you know me. Lord, how can I know you better?

Thank you Lord that you love me. Lord, how can I love you more?

Finish by thanking and worshipping him, even if you're uncertain that what you've written down is from the Lord. You can read through it straight away, or put it aside to review later. It may be instantly clear that God has spoken to you, or it may take time to sink in and digest.

Answers from God come in many different forms, and the answer may come straight away—or hours, days or even weeks later. And it may not come in a way you expect. God can and does communicate in all kinds of ways, just as we do in everyday life. In scripture there are examples of God speaking audibly, through an angel, a prophet, a vision, a dream, the weather, a budding almond branch—even a donkey. So as you listen for his voice, cast aside any preconceived notions, limitations or barriers. You are embarking on an adventure.

As you get used to dialogue with God and to recognizing his voice, you can go deeper with your questions (see the next chapter). God is so amazing, so wonderful, that you will never reach the end of discovering the height, width and depth of his love.

Listening in a group

Although these five steps can be done on your own, there are benefits to doing it in a small group. There are two ways to do this: the leader could ask the group to carry out the steps at home, then bring their answers to share at the next meeting. Or the group could go through the steps together, listening to

God individually in silence or with background music, and then sharing answers with each other as they feel comfortable.

In our home church, often the answers people received didn't seem to make much sense to them, but as we discussed them in the group, these seemingly unrelated answers were in fact the very answer that another member had been seeking. This happened many, many times. We also learnt that when you do get an answer from the Lord, often it's an answer for everyone. Somehow a personal answer that's meant just for you speaks to someone else about their situation too, even though they are completely unrelated. That's one of the blessings about sharing in a small group of trusted friends.

14.

Going Deeper

However, as it is written:

"What no eye has seen,

what no ear has heard,

and what no human mind has conceived"

—the things God has prepared for those who love him—

these are the things God has revealed to us by his Spirit.

1 Corinthians 2:9-10a

***

As you get used to being still before God, worshipping him and hearing his voice, you can explore his character and relationship more deeply. Two areas are especially worth focusing on: love and purpose.

Love

> If I speak in the tongues of men or of angels,
> but do not have love, I am only a resounding
> gong or a clanging cymbal. If I have the gift of
> prophecy and can fathom all mysteries and all
> knowledge, and if I have a faith that can move
> mountains, but do not have love, I am nothing.
> If I give all I possess to the poor and give over
> my body to hardship that I may boast, but do
> not have love, I gain nothing.
>
> 1 Corinthians 13:1-3

Love is always the benchmark that we return to since all the gifts and plans God gives us revolve around love. Love is the proof that God is working in our lives: the more we love, the more we are being transformed, and the more effective we will be.

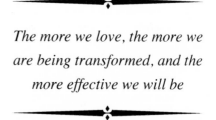

The more we love, the more we are being transformed, and the more effective we will be

Listening for God's love

You can start with the five steps to listen to God's voice as outlined in the previous chapter. For worship, choose songs that focus on expressing love for God. As the music plays, write out in your own words what it is you love about him. Think about each member of the Trinity. What is it you see when you meditate on each one? Make three very specific lists—Father, Son and Holy Spirit—list each characteristic or thing they have done. Then use the list as your worship—thanking God for each point, such as, "Thank you Jesus for the pain you went through on the cross for me" and "Thank you Holy Spirit for living inside me and being my counselor."

After each point, pause to give God room to respond. Remember to give and receive, give and receive, just like a normal human conversation.

Pray, "I ask you, Lord, to open the eyes of my heart that I may know you more."

Then try asking some or all of the following questions, and write out what you receive:

"Lord, would you show me your love?"

"Lord, how can I experience more of your love?"

"Lord, is anything in my life blocking me from receiving more of your love?"

Purpose

Relationship with God is the main purpose of Christianity, more than anything we can *do* for God. And from relationship springs purpose. So when you prepare to listen to God, you are listening with purpose. I know that at the end of my days I will stand before him and give an account of what I've done in my life, and I don't want to stand before him empty-handed. It always amazes me when I ask believers what God's plan is for their life, and many of them have absolutely no idea because they haven't even asked him.

God has a clear and defined plan for your life, "plans to prosper you and not harm you" (Jer 29:11). Could it be that you haven't asked about these plans, callings and gifts from the Lord? Take some time and ask him about these. Continue to ask about them on a regular basis and write down everything that you hear, or draw the images that come to your mind.

Listening for God's purpose

Read the scripture below from Jeremiah out loud at least three times. Read it once normally then pause. Read it again very slowly then pause again. Read it a third time, placing the emphasis differently. Then read the prayer that follows.

> "For I know the plans I have for you," declares the Lord, "plans to prosper you and not to harm you, plans to give you hope and a future. Then you will call on me and come and pray to me, and I will listen to you. You will seek me and find me when you seek me with all your heart."

> Jeremiah 29:11-13

"Holy Spirit make your words truth in my life.
Holy Spirit make your words come alive in
my life.
Holy Spirit make your words reality in my life.
Amen."

Take a moment to just pause and give the Lord space to comment on this. Write down anything that comes to mind.

Then try asking some or all of the following questions, and write out the answers. Write down what you receive word for word—the very first things that pop into your head. It's critically important that you do not over-think the thoughts that jump into your mind immediately. As before, don't try to evaluate yet, just get a flow going. If you honestly don't get anything, be patient. Don't give up.

"Lord, how can I seek you with all my heart?"

"Lord, tell me about your plans for my life."

"Lord, how can I increase my faith?"

"Lord, how can I cooperate with your plans?"

"Lord, how are you revealing yourself to me through your plan unfolding in my life?"

"Lord, what is the most important part of yourself that you are trying to show me in this season?"

After your time of listening and dialogue has finished, look back at what you've written to start discerning if you've heard from God or not.

How do I know it's really God's voice?

> Do not quench the Spirit. Do not treat prophecies with contempt but test them all; hold on to what is good…
>
> 1 Thessalonians 5:19-21

Many people ask me how to tell if it's really God speaking to them, or just their own voice, or something else. This is a very important question which could take many more books to explain but I will try to simplify it here.

God's voice is different from our own internal thoughts

God's voice often comes as a sudden thought that just drops into your heart without warning, and it is often accompanied by a deep conviction from the Holy Spirit; a feeling of wonder and awe.

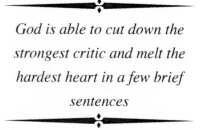

God is able to cut down the strongest critic and melt the hardest heart in a few brief sentences

However, it may not be that easy to discern God's voice, especially when you are new to listening to him. Sometimes

God's voice can feel like a thought that you came up with all by yourself, but one indication that it's really from God is that the thought is totally unexpected: perhaps it's a word or phrase that you wouldn't normally use; a picture that you have never imagined before; an idea that has never occurred to you before; or a passage of scripture that just popped into your head when you weren't thinking of anything remotely similar.

His voice usually arrives as a completely, fully formed thought, rather than a developing or evolving thought. I personally tend to speak in a roundabout fashion and eventually get to my point after circling it a few times. God isn't like this—he is very succinct. Just read how Jesus communicated in the gospels. God is able to cut down the strongest critic and melt the hardest heart in a few brief sentences.

In my experience, God's thoughts are dropped into my mind so quickly that there is no possible way that I could have thought of them myself. It's like an instant download of blue prints for a sculpture or an innovative idea. Often the response comes so fast that you couldn't possibly have had time to think it up yourself.

And if you only ever hear thoughts that agree with your own ideas and points of view you are probably hearing from yourself, not God. God's ideas are often contrary to society's point of view—and our own. He is in agreement with himself, and just as he was at odds with the society in the time of Jesus, he is even more so now. And if you are hearing directions which are clearly opposite to what the Bible says, then you are not hearing from God.

Discerning God's voice takes commitment and time

Write down everything you believe God is telling you since often his thoughts are very quick and fleeting. It's similar to dreams—once you wake up it's almost impossible to remember them unless you write them down immediately. God often talks through dreams, so it's a very good habit to keep your notebook and pen beside your bed. If you don't capture God's thoughts at the exact moment you get them then they are often gone, sometimes forever.

Many times when words or images are from the Lord, you will see depths of meaning over time that weren't obvious at the beginning. When you read the Bible, you will see connections which will ring true for you or not. He has an amazing ability to speak in layers that unfold over time, in different ways at different times in your life. Every relationship is built over time and building a relationship with God is no different. The pursuit of God, and learning to recognize his voice, is a lifetime endeavour.

Whenever you aren't 100 percent sure that something is from God, then ask him for confirmation. When God really wants to talk with you about something he isn't short on ways to do it. He is very able to confirm his word through scriptures, prophetic words from others, signs in nature, through dreams, and many other ways.

Correction versus condemnation

One of the most common problems I've seen in listening to God is confusing *correction* and *condemnation*. God corrects those he loves (Heb 12:6, Prov 3:12) and he has sent the Holy Spirit to bring conviction of sin (John 16:8). So if you never get corrected as you listen to God, that could be a warning sign that you are not hearing him accurately; and similarly if all you receive is correction, that too suggests that something in your heart is not right.

However, there is a huge, and I mean huge, difference between correction and condemnation. Jesus has come to the world not to condemn but to save (John 12:47). A condemning "word" brings discouragement instead of freedom. If the voice or message you hear is accusing, critical, or threatening, or puts bar-

When God really wants to talk with you about something he isn't short on ways to do it

riers between people, then you can know immediately that it's not from God. Correction, on the other hand, is a doorway to freedom. Correction is the truth that will set you free. This is why you can celebrate when the Lord corrects you, because he's giving you a map to get out of some problem that has oppressed you.

God's word promotes holy living and develops the fruit of the Holy Spirit: love, joy, peace, patience, kindness, goodness and faithfulness (Gal 5:22). Any word "from God" that is not in accordance with the fruit of the Spirit, or promotes sin, is clearly wrong.

Lining up with scripture

Most important of all—what you receive from God needs to be aligned with scripture. Therefore, the better you know scripture the better you'll be able to discern this for yourself. Studying scripture will always be of benefit to you. I encourage you to not only study the Bible but to search it for the heart of God.

Blockages to hearing God's voice

If you've tried the five steps outlined in the previous chapter and tried to go deeper into hearing God's voice, and you are still finding it hard to hear his voice, you may need to explore whether there is some kind of blockage in your heart. There are some common blockages for people to hearing from God, or hearing accurately. This chapter isn't long enough for an in-depth analysis on this topic, but let's try to hit a few of the main points.

Unacknowledged sin

In a nutshell, sin separates us from God. Jesus dealt with all our sin on the cross, allowing us into relationship with a holy God; but we still have to deal with sin on a daily basis. If we don't actively acknowledge our sin and take it to the cross, it hampers communication with God: "If I had cherished sin in my heart, the Lord would not have listened" (Ps 66:18). Repentance, confession, and receiving the forgiveness that the Lord longs to give us clears the way to hear from him again.

Unforgiveness

You may be holding onto unforgiveness towards yourself and/or others. If you don't think you have anyone to forgive, then you may need to think again—ask God to show you (write down the names of those people who come to mind). Remember that "getting over something", which tends to happen over time, is not the same as forgiving. Forgiving is a choice, often in spite of our feelings. Forgiveness is not optional for believers—we forgive because God has forgiven us. We must lead a life of continual forgiveness, from the idiot who cut you off in traffic, to the person who truly, deeply hurt you.

If God has shown you there's someone you need to forgive, here's a practical way to do it. First, acknowledge how hurt you are—tell the Lord out loud exactly what the person has done to you and, importantly, how it made you feel. It's ok to be angry—that's a normal human emotion. You may need to shed some tears so get the tissues ready. Next, declare out loud that you forgive that person, say their name, give up your right to judge them, and hand them over to God. Be specific on what you forgive them for. Then pray that God will bless that person. It's important that you speak this forgiveness out loud and not just silently in your head.

When you truly forgive someone, even when they don't deserve it, it sets you (and them) free. This is an incredibly powerful spiritual principle, and this critical process will likely help you hear God's voice much clearer as a result.

Lack of faith

Lack of faith is a real blockage to hearing the voice of God for some people. There are many believers who just don't believe that God can or would speak to them, and they explain away everything that God does as coincidence. If you find yourself doing this, but are still hungry to hear his voice, try building your faith through Step 4 in the previous chapter—reading aloud the statements about God wanting to speak to you.

Unresolved hurts

Unresolved hurts and pain from the past can and do have an effect on hearing accurately from God. Dealing with past hurts is separate from forgiveness (although forgiveness is often a crucial part of it). This is about coming out from under the influence of the past hurts that tend to project themselves into the present. Deep wounds can be like a pair of colored glasses that tint everything you see, often without you being aware of this. You may need to talk and pray them through with a counselor, church leader or another mature Christian you trust. There are also some excellent Christian self-help books on this topic.

Wrong beliefs about God

So many people believe—though not always consciously—that God is distant, angry or vengeful. If this is your belief, you will have constant storm clouds brewing over everything you hear. But scripture clearly states that God sent his Son to earth because of his love (John 3:16): God's love is his most defining characteristic. Difficult circumstances in your life do not prove that he is punishing you; God is with you through all the trials and will be with you to the end, using them to help you become a better person. A good way forward is to search the Bible for declarations of his love. Write out those verses, personalising them with 'me' and 'I', and read them to yourself every day. The better you understand his character, the more easily you will recognize his voice.

Active listening

Here is a final challenge for you. "Active listening" is a term I use to describe an attitude of listening that goes past designated prayer times to encompass your whole life. Do you believe that God wants to communicate with you anywhere and everywhere? Could your faith stretch to believing that he has a *lot* to say to you?

Psalm 139 is wonderful for showing us a God who knows us intimately, and whose Spirit is with us everywhere; anywhere you could possibly go, God is already there ahead of you. Take time to read, or better still to memorize, these words:

> O Lord, you have examined my heart
> and know everything about me.
> You know when I sit down or stand up.
> You know my thoughts even when I'm far away.
> You see me when I travel
> and when I rest at home.
> You know everything I do.
> You know what I am going to say
> even before I say it, Lord.
> You go before me and follow me.
> You place your hand of blessing on my head.
> Such knowledge is too wonderful for me,
> too great for me to understand!
> I can never escape from your Spirit!
> I can never get away from your presence!
> If I go up to heaven, you are there;
> if I go down to the grave, you are there.
> If I ride the wings of the morning,
> if I dwell by the farthest oceans,
> even there your hand will guide me,
> and your strength will support me.
> I could ask the darkness to hide me

and the light around me to become night—
but even in darkness I cannot hide from you.
To you the night shines as bright as day.
Darkness and light are the same to you.
You made all the delicate, inner parts of my body
and knit me together in my mother's womb.
Thank you for making me so wonderfully
complex!
Your workmanship is marvelous—how well I
know it.
You watched me as I was being formed in utter
seclusion,
as I was woven together in the dark of the womb.
You saw me before I was born.
Every day of my life was recorded in your book.
Every moment was laid out
before a single day had passed.
How precious are your thoughts about
me, O God.
They cannot be numbered!
I can't even count them;
they outnumber the grains of sand!
And when I wake up,
you are still with me!

Psalm 139:1-18, New Living Translation

God's thoughts about you "outnumber the grains of sand". Just for fun, I thought I'd try to estimate the number of grains of sand on the earth (it's amazing what you can find on the internet.) Anyway the best guess I found was 3,000,000,000,000... up to 29 zeroes.[2] And the scripture says that his thoughts about you outnumber them! That means that if you live to an average age of 80 years, giving you about 2.5 billion seconds of life, God would have more than 27,452 thoughts towards you per *second*, every second, for your entire life. To tune into a few thoughts, or even 10 to 20 thoughts from the Lord each day, would be merely the tiniest of drops in the ocean of his thoughts.

So now I ask you, is God distant, indifferent and silent? Or is he deeply involved in the very details of your life, thinking deeply and sharing his thoughts with you?

Being with God all day, every day

As you are going about your day today, and over the next few days, try to take a few quiet moments in different locations for some active listening to what God has to say. The idea here is to start to include the Lord in your daily activities.

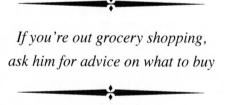

If you're out grocery shopping, ask him for advice on what to buy

---

Worship is always a good way to start, so put on your ear buds when you are doing the laundry, or listen to music in your car. Recite part of Psalm 139 from memory and thank God for all the thoughts he has about you. Have a look around you, and find something that you can praise him for. Praise him for the sunshine, or for the people you work with, or whatever comes to mind. Then just ask him some questions. If you're out grocery shopping, ask him for advice on what to buy. Then don't forget to listen to what he says! Try and get a dialogue going on whatever is happening around you. Be creative, and don't worry about where you are—he is already there ahead of you.

A final prayer

Finally—I hope that this book has inspired you to develop a deep, daily relationship with God. I'll leave you with this prayer as a way to come into God's presence, and to simply be with him. May God richly bless you as you spend time with him.

> Lord Jesus, sweet Jesus, your name is like
> honey on my lips, your Spirit is like water to
> my soul; I worship you and honor you.
> Through your blood I enter into your presence.
> You are my everything, my all in all. You are
> the beginning and the end, by you and through
> you all things are made. Holy Spirit come to

me, let me breathe you in, fill me up with your presence and transform me.

Wash me, cleanse me, and forgive me, oh Lord. You surround me and go before me. You protect me with your mighty arm. You fill me with wisdom. You are a light on my path.

I am filled with love, overflowing with joy, and surrounded by peace. Your goodness, kindness, gentleness and patience flow through me.

Lord, I receive who you are into my innermost being; thank you that by your grace I am saved, healed and set free.

I receive your plans and purposes, your gifts and callings for my life. Use me for the building of your kingdom here in this world. May your will be fully and completely accomplished in my life.

Let me be one who hears your voice, who sees your glory, and who understands your wisdom. Let your light shine through me.

I receive right now all your anointing and empowering of your Spirit to fulfil your calling on my life. I receive the impartation to *be* with you all the days of my life.

Amen.

Has this book blessed you?
I'd love to hear your story.
Share your own journey of learning to BE with God.
Visit my ministry website for more content, video messages
and teaching on how you can breakthrough to
a supernatural life.

***

If you would like to contact Franklyn Spence or invite
him for a speaking engagement, please contact him via his
ministry website or on Facebook.
www.forerunner-ministries.com
Facebook: Forerunner Ministries Franklyn Spence

***

To learn more about the art work of Franklyn Spence
please visit his personal website.
www.franklynspence.com

CPSIA information can be obtained
at www.ICGtesting.com
Printed in the USA
LVOW11s0540220617
538962LV00001B/95/P